Passing Through the Fire

Author Contact Information

Nasrin can be contacted by email
at passingthroughthefire@gmail.com

To view Nasrin's art work, visit her
Facebook page "passing through the fire"

Passing Through the Fire
Pathway to Freedom

Nasrin Z.

iUniverse, Inc.
Bloomington

Passing Through The Fire
Pathway to Freedom

Unless otherwise indicated, all Scripture quotations are taken from the New International Version of the Bible.

iUniverse books may be ordered through booksellers or by contacting:

iUniverse
1663 Liberty Drive
Bloomington, IN 47403
www.iuniverse.com
1-800-Authors (1-800-288-4677)

ISBN: 978-1-4697-8751-0 (sc)
ISBN: 978-1-4697-8752-7 (ebk)

Printed in the United States of America

iUniverse rev. date: 03/06/2012

*Dedicated to all who comforted me
in times of my greatest need.*

In our desperation,
when the depth of darkness sees no end,
and death casts its shadow on our days,
while pain besieges our souls,
our only hope in hopelessness
is the merciful and forgiving God.
He illuminates our path,
and enlightens our hearts.

Shahram Z.

Life is empty, bleak, and hopeless
without faith in God.

Nasrin Z.

Contents

Preface

We are living in a world of adversity. It is all around us. It is universal. It is impossible to avoid, and it can strike at any time. On a cold December day in 1997, while driving to work in Atlanta, I was involved in a car accident that rendered me a quadriplegic. Suddenly paralyzed, I found that life as I had known it was over; my goals and dreams were shattered. Bewildered by this sudden life-changing event, a lingering thought haunted me: "Where was God in all of this?" Born into a Muslim family in Iran, I had converted to Christianity just a few years prior to my accident.

Through my journey of many deep and dark valleys, I discovered the love, presence, and provision of God, and found a renewed sense of purpose. While our goals and dreams may be shattered, there is a real supernatural power from above that will empower us to endure the storms of life and assures us that all things are leading us to the right destination. Although it has been cathartic to tell my story, my purpose for writing this book is to help you discover this Love as well.

While this story seems to be about me, it is not. It's about the grace and the transforming power of God. Looking through the window of my life, you too will see the footprints of God.

Some of the names have been changed or omitted to protect the privacy of individuals.

1

Whisper of the Wind

Remember this moment

It was a cool October afternoon in 1997. I finished my work early and headed home from downtown Atlanta. As a busy tax accountant, it was unusual for me to leave work early, especially since our tax season deadline was soon approaching. Once home, I changed into comfortable clothes and walked down the deck towards the backyard. I loved this house that we had purchased just three years earlier. It was a two-story home with a double deck that sloped down to a wooded backyard, ending at the bank of a bubbling creek. There were no fences separating the neighborhood homes and no visible houses behind us, only woods.

The lush summer leaves had now transformed to vibrant colors of red and deep orange. Blue Jays and red Cardinals were frequent visitors to feed on the seeds from the bird-house in our yard. At dawn, the croaking of frogs rising from the creek played like a musical ensemble, while fireflies lit up the night like Christmas lights.

I climbed into the hammock hung between two oak trees. The sun was still warm to the skin as I began reading a book. A chipmunk searching for food stopped and looked around before it plunged back into the woods. A sudden rush of cool air overtook me, and with the book on my chest, I closed my eyes. I heard a gentle voice within me whispering, "*Remember this moment.*" My mind focused on the sound of water rushing through the creek, the scent of wild flowers waving in the breeze, and the singing of the birds. The memories were etched into my mind.

A disturbing thought suddenly interrupted the serenity of the moment: "Why must I remember this moment?" What I didn't know, was that this would be the last time I would enjoy lying on the hammock in our backyard. Dark clouds were soon approaching, and a raging storm was upon me.

❦   ❦   ❦

It was now late November. My husband, Shahram, and I, with the help of a friend, spent the weekend planting 50 daffodil bulbs in our front yard, so they would blossom bright yellow next spring. Shahram had bought two packages of daffodil bulbs on sale. Whenever he saw a good deal, he would always buy two, one for us, and one for a friend. We ended that day dining with our friend and reading poetry written by ancient Persian poets.[1] Literature is my husband's passion. In his library, you will find collections of books ranging from ancient Persian poets to contemporary authors. Poetry recitation is a traditional Iranian pastime that we both enjoyed. Over the centuries, despite foreign invasions, the Persian culture and language were kept alive through the

---

[1]   The name Persia was changed to Iran in 1935.

poems written by the Persian poets.[2] We selected a poem to recite, written by Rumi, a 13th century mystical Persian poet. Afterwards, we cleaned up the kitchen. It was late when our friend left, and I finally went to bed that night. Before falling asleep, my mind drifted to the events that had brought my husband and me to this place. We were both born in Iran; our paths crossed and were blended when we met in America.

---

[2] Persian poets such as Ferdowsi, Sa'di, Hafiz, Rumi and Omar Khayyam are well known in the West and have influenced the literature of many countries.

2

Blended Paths

*There are lessons to be found in every event in
our lives.*

I was born in Tehran, into a family of three sisters and
one brother. My father, if he wasn't working at his job, was
tending to "his garden." He loved his garden in our courtyard,
which had all sorts of fruit trees, herbs and vegetables. My
mother, like most women of her era, was a homemaker.
She managed everything and encouraged us girls to be
independent. And when she ran out of things to do, she
would look for a new hobby, from using a German-made
knitting machine to create sweaters, to making artificial
flowers using all sorts of gadgets.

My younger sister and I were like twins. They called
our names in unison, Nasrin and Simin, as if we came
in a package! My mom even dressed us alike. Simin was
energetic and sociable and I was the shy and quiet one.
We did everything together. We rode our bikes in the
neighborhood after school, played in snow in the winters,
and during occasional spring showers, danced in the rain
outside before coming home to a cup of warm Persian tea
and biscuits our grandma prepared for us.

My grandmother, who was widowed years before I was born, lived with us. I loved my grandma and will always remember her wrinkled face and her long white hair plaited down her back. She had great reverence for God, and when we were young children, she taught us the daily Muslim prayers. With the aid of a magnifying glass, she would read the newspapers every day, commenting that the wars and famines were signs that the end of the world was near.[3] The rest of my family were nominal Moslems, with the exception of my mother who to this day won't miss her daily Namaz, the Muslim's prayer.

My childhood memories take me back to our quiet, suburban neighborhood, north of Tehran. It was one of the planned neighborhoods of Tehran, with its numbered streets and newly built houses. The streams of water ran through shallow canals from north to south, and mulberry trees lined the main street. I walked those streets every day to get to school. Our family vacations were spent north of Tehran near the Caspian Sea. The Caspian coastline with its sandy beaches, lush vegetation, and spectacular natural scenery was a popular vacation destination. I remember riding in our family car around the huge mountains, through the natural tunnels where the air suddenly changed to cool and crisp, as we watched for the sea to appear on the other side. Life was simpler then, and Iran seemed like the safest place on earth. Under the Shah's regime, Iran was a radically different country than what it is now.[4]

---

[3]   Islam and Christianity predict somewhat similar "end-time" events but with different outcomes.

[4]   Mohammad Reza Shah Pahlavi was the king of Iran from 1941to1979.

When my older sister, Fari, got married, she and her husband traveled to America, where he studied petroleum engineering at the University of Oklahoma. At that time, Iran and the United States had close economic, social, and political ties. Iranian students who wanted to study petroleum engineering were flooding the universities in Texas, Louisiana, or Oklahoma. Their goal was to return to Iran and work in prestigious positions for the Iranian National Oil Company.

Considering education to be of utmost importance, Iranians were sending their younger children to study in schools all over the world. It was a good opportunity for them to learn the language and the culture, and acquire a fine education abroad. So one by one, we came. I left Iran and came to America in December of 1974. I was only 15 years old, and too young to wonder about an unknown tomorrow. I never imagined when I left the Mehrabad Airport in Tehran that I would never again see the land of my birth.

I stayed with my sister, Fari, and her family in Oklahoma while attending high school. My first impression in high school was that America was not only the land of the free, but also the land of the giants! I was quite petite, and sixteen-year-old boys at my school were bigger and taller than any man I had ever seen in Iran.

Although I was taught English from the first grade in Iran, I soon realized I couldn't understand anything! But it wasn't too long before "y'all" and "gosh darnit" became a part of my everyday vocabulary. So, I speak English with a Persian accent and a Southern twist. I found schools in America much more fun than in Iran; the football games, the homecoming festivities, and the social hour activities made coping with homesickness a little easier.

After graduating from high school, I began studying at the University of Oklahoma. Influenced by my favorite professor, I decided to major in psychology. The study of the human mind intrigued me, and I was captivated by the TV images of a therapist listening to people revealing their most intimate inner thoughts. I enjoyed my studies, and found myself particularly interested in the study of abnormal psychology, psychotic disorders that cause abnormal thinking and perception and loss of touch with reality. I took every course that was available in that field.

The late seventies in America was the era of the disco subculture, popularized by movies like "Saturday Night Fever," and was characterized by flashy music and shimmering fashion. So when I wasn't studying, I was at the parties, the rock concerts, the disco clubs, living the carefree days of youth. However, I soon realized that the world we live in wasn't a carefree place at all! Dramatic changes were happening in my homeland. In 1978, the Iranian Revolution began. I was startled watching the events unfold on the television news. "How could this be happening in my beautiful country? Why a religious revolution?" I often asked. In 1979, the video "The Late Great Planet Earth" was released, depicting the apocalyptic vision of the end of the world based on interpretation of Biblical prophecies.[5] Watching this film and the events in Iran began an intense, soul-searching journey for me. My world no longer seemed secure. I could hear the voice of my grandmother echoing, "The signs of the end times, famines and wars . . . !"

In the midst of the confusion and conflict of conscience, I immersed myself in religion in search of answers. However, the deeper I plunged into Islam, my religion, the

---

[5] *The Late, Great Planet Earth,* co-authored by Hal Lindsey and Carole C. Carlson, was adapted in 1979 into a movie narrated by Orson Welles.

further I found myself drifting from God. My search did not lead to an inner peace or a true inner change of attitude; I just appeared religious. I had become a stranger to myself! Disillusioned, I abandoned religion altogether.

In mid-January 1979, the Shah left Iran for exile, and two weeks later the exiled Ayatollah Khomeini returned to Tehran to be greeted by several million Iranians. The royal regime collapsed shortly thereafter, and it was voted by national referendum for Iran to become an Islamic Republic on April 1, 1979. The monarchy that had governed Iran for my whole life was replaced with an Islamic republic under Ayatollah Khomeini. On November 4, 1979, a group of Islamist students and militants took over the American Embassy in Tehran and held the Americans who worked there hostage for 444 days. The hostage crisis caused many Iranians who lived abroad to experience blatant prejudice and outright hostility.

Expecting freedom and equality from the revolution, all hope was shattered when the inequality of women became the rule in our homeland. Women were forced to observe the Islamic dress code and were subjected to fines, sentenced to prison, and many suffered beatings for disobedience. The Islamic government strictly enforced segregation of the sexes, from schools to ski slopes, and even public buses. The revolution brought with it a governmental promotion of Islamic laws. Until then, the government had not enforced the Islamic religion, and people of different religions had lived peacefully together in Iran.

I had been somewhat naïve about the injustice that existed in the world, but now my eyes were wide open. My heart was in a perpetual state of longing, sadness and fear for my family who were still living in Iran, especially when the Iran-Iraq war began in September of 1980. Often, I wondered what their daily lives were like. The horrible pictures and news coming out of Iran kept my emotions trapped in a state of despair. I plunged into my studies and managed to graduate from college; however, a lack of purpose and direction led to an overwhelming sense of emptiness. Perhaps it had always been there, but I became more conscious of it then.

Following the revolution, many Iranians opted to remain in the U.S. and become naturalized citizens, including myself. After months of aimlessly searching for employment, I moved to Houston, where my brother and his family lived. I became proficient with computers, and was finally able to get an office job. With encouragement from management, I enrolled at the University of Houston to study accounting, while working full time, and later became a Certified Public Accountant.

Having found a new purpose, things seemed to be going well except for the loneliness. Before the Iran-Iraq war ended, my parents were able to leave Iran for America, and finally, after so many years we were once again reunited. Words cannot describe the emotional and exciting reunion. There was much joy and relief to have them near us and out of harm's way. They settled in Oklahoma where my older sister lived.

During the spring of 1989, I was working full time and volunteering for an Iranian radio station in town. (Houston had a large concentration of Iranian population that led to the emergence of many businesses, media and cultural institutions.) One day, while working at the radio station, I answered a phone call from a man in the listening audience. He asked whether he could show his slides from his recent trip to Iran at an Iranian New Year's party we were organizing. (The Iranian New Year is on March 21, the first day of spring.) His name was Shahram, and we arranged to meet to select the appropriate slides.

Shahram and I shared some serious conversation, as well as much laughter the day we met. He revealed the reason why he was in Houston; he had accompanied his younger brother, who had flown from Iran to the Texas Medical Center, where he had heart surgery to repair a rare childhood condition. His operation had been a success, and he had returned to Iran after his recovery. Shahram remained in Houston, and he planned to move to another state sometime in the future.

I found him to be very intelligent and funny. His dark hair and piercing blue eyes made him unusually handsome. We also shared the same interest in psychology, which made conversing with him so familiar and comfortable. Soon we were seeing each other virtually every day and talking on the phone three or four times a day. A deep soul connection developed between us.

Through the weeks, Shahram and I talked about his life. After graduating from high school in Iran, he moved to America and began studying at a college in Oklahoma. After one year, he moved to Louisiana, where he earned his graduate degree in petroleum engineering from the University of South Western Louisiana. He then worked a few years in the U.S. before returning to Iran. In 1984, he flew to Germany, purchased a brand new Mercedes Benz, and took a long road trip to the majestic city of Prague in Czech Republic (Czechoslovakia at that time). His brother joined him there, and they traveled through Turkey to Iran. During his travels, this free-spirited man mingled with the locals and was invited to their homes; he ate at the sidewalk cafes in the fairy-tale city of Prague, and played backgammon in the seashore restaurants of Istanbul.

It was during the turbulent time of war when he returned to Iran. How can one begin to detail the consequences of war? Among the many destructive effects is the suffering that civilians experience. But more than that, Shahram was numbed by the atrocity, injustice, and oppression he witnessed by the Iranian government against its own people in the streets of Tehran. Two years later, realizing that he had become a stranger to the beloved country he once knew, he decided to return to the United States. However, when he applied for permission to do so, the government of Iran denied him permission to exit. Determined to leave, he crossed the treacherous mountains to escape to Turkey, but he was captured and imprisoned by the Iranian Revolutionary Guard.

He was thrown into an old prison cell with other inmates. Looking at the gloomy faces of the inmates crammed into a dark, small room, he told them in a cool manner, "Gentlemen, you don't seem to be very content with your life here!" He immediately won their friendship with his wit. But the Revolutionary Guards who interrogated him didn't care much about his humor, and they suspected he was a member of the "Mujahedin," a religious leftist organization that advocated the overthrow of the Islamic Republic of Iran. During the interrogations, he was beaten and tortured. When his parents became aware of his whereabouts, they rushed to his aid and made up a bizarre story to convince the guards to eventually release him.

With broken ribs and a broken nose, soon after his recovery, Shahram tried to leave Iran again. Fleeing to freedom, as he was crossing the mountains, he reached a barley field. He had to spend an entire day in the field hiding from the guards. As he lay silently in a seemingly endless golden field, with the warm breeze gently swaying the barley grains, he noticed ants busily picking up the crushed barley and crossing over his body to go to their destination. Perhaps his purpose for that day was to help feed the ants, he thought. Gazing up at the sky, he noticed a light shining through the clouds. Suddenly, he felt as if he was in a palm of a giant hand and heard a small voice within saying, "Everything will be all right." That night, as he was crossing the mountain, he was caught in a barrage of gunfire from the Revolutionary Guards, but none of the bullets hit him, and after several days, he made it safely to Turkey and then on to the United States.

Fortunately, the ravages of war did not dampen his sense of humor. Although at times it was a bit twisted, he would always make me laugh. He was a welcome change in my mundane and structured life. We were soul mates in love and were soon married in the courthouse, just the two of us, on December 1, 1989. We met downtown and walked to the courthouse that day. I was wearing my cream color suit and he wore a dark three-piece suit. The lady at the courthouse led us to the Judge's office through a long underground tunnel, which she called "The tunnel of no return!" We both laughed.

". . . in sickness and in health till death do you part?" "I do." I don't think either of us understood the significance of those vows at the time, and how hard it could become to live them well!

During our first year of marriage, we spent intimate hours engaged in deep conversations about Shahram's adventurous escape from Iran, an experience that impacted the rest of his life. I listened intently to every detail. There are lessons to be found in every event in our lives. He learned about love when a little boy, seeing him lost and hungry in the mountains, brought him bread from the nearby village. He learned about evil when he was tortured at the hands of his captors. He learned about loneliness when his guides scattered during a raid by the border police, left him in the deep of night in the unfamiliar terrain of mountains. He learned about hope when he finally crossed the border into Turkey and to freedom. And he learned about joy through tears when he was united with his family waiting for him in Turkey. The painful experience of being captured and tortured in Iran also left deep scars on Shahram's soul, which became apparent to me a few years after our marriage.

We decided from the beginning not to have children. Neither of us felt that we wanted that level of responsibility. For me, raising children was serious business. I thought of people who wanted to have kids as brave, and I did not see myself as a very brave person.

I landed a job in the tax department of Shell Oil Company headquartered in the heart of downtown Houston. Looking back, the extensive training and skill development I received provided me with skills that helped me throughout my career and beyond. The conferences held in various cities across the U.S. gave my husband and me a chance to vacation in some interesting cities, and brought a level of excitement to an otherwise typical accounting job.

A year after our marriage, my dad suddenly passed away. We were devastated! I stayed with my mom for a few days at my parents' home in Oklahoma, where they had lived for years. We celebrated every holiday there, from the Iranian New Year to Christmas. The neighborhood was built around a large private lake. During the Christmas holidays, the magical reflection of lights on the water made the neighborhood a local attraction. My dad had planted his garden in the backyard, and after every visit he would send me home with a large basket of fresh basil and mint. Their homemade yogurt and freshly baked bread were among my favorite treats.

While staying with my mom after the funeral, I awoke one day to the quacking of ducks in the backyard. I put on my robe and walked down to the edge of the lake. The sun was rising and the water reflected warm hues of orange and yellow across the water. The grass under my feet felt damp from the morning dew. Near the lake, flocks of ducks and geese were walking on the grass and some came closer to the house and started knocking with their beaks on the window of the outside patio door. Every morning, at sunrise, my dad fed the birds, and now they were looking for him. They retreated when I tried to feed them, and one by one they flew away. It was as though they knew he wouldn't be coming back. My dad was a lover of nature and nature loved him back. Although he is gone, he will never leave that tender place in my heart.

3

Encounter with God

*There comes a time when we are finally
ready to have a deep encounter with God's Spirit
that will forever change our lives.*

A few years into our marriage, difficulties began. As
with most marriages, we discovered that we were just so
different! Also, I saw a bitterness in Shahram that sometimes
turned to anger, which I couldn't understand. Attempts to
communicate with him only met with sarcasm, indifference
or criticism. The turmoil drove us apart and threatened
our relationship. My illusion of a perfect marriage was
shattered.

In the spring of 1993, a friend, knowing my marital
difficulties, invited me to a marriage seminar at a church. I
was disillusioned with religion, so turning to God was the
farthest thought from my mind. Nonetheless, God is always
ready to draw near and fill this void.

Upon examining my life, even during times when I felt
I had everything needed to be happy, there was a void. It
is this void that is exploited by the media. They point out
our inadequacies to convince us that the solution is what
they have to offer. I tried to fill this void in many ways,
thinking that worldly pleasures would satisfy the longing

within me that only God could fill. Looking back, I can see many times when God was gently calling me, but I was not ready to listen. A few weeks after arriving in America, a fellow high school student gave me a Persian Bible, but I was not ready to read it. I was invited to a few churches and heard impressive messages, but I was not ready to receive. I had many unusual encounters with God, but was not yet ready to respond. I was not looking for God—but God was looking for me!

I believed in the existence of God, but had come to a place in my life, where God was simply irrelevant. In fact, I would only call on the name of God when a disaster was about to happen. Despite our resistance, there comes a time when we are finally ready to experience a deep encounter with God's Spirit that will forever change our lives.

A friend introduced me to a group of Iranian Christians, who had converted from Islam. They had no church building and met in each other's homes. They claimed to have a personal relationship with God! Their enthusiasm and sincerity of faith drew me near. They prayed to God as a spiritual father and sang songs of worship to Him. At first, participating in singing and praying seemed unfamiliar and strange, but I soon found my soul penetrated by the profound lyrics and lovely melodies.

In this small community of Christians from different walks of life, I saw a joy I couldn't explain and a hope that I didn't understand. For them, God was real, relevant, and active in their everyday lives. They prayed fervently, gave thanksgiving for their blessings, and served one another compassionately. They claimed God spoke to them. I was completely baffled! "The God who is beyond approach would speak to us?" "How is that possible?" I always thought we humans are too trivial for His consideration. "Would God ever speak to me?" I felt a deep desire to know this God. Recognizing this nagging emptiness, a void, a spiritual hunger in my life, I was willing to listen. I visited other churches and heard testimonies of restored marriages, recovered addicts, and mended hearts. I saw changed lives! I began attending church regularly.

❦ ❦ ❦

Soon after, I accepted a job offer in Atlanta. We thought relocating would be good for our marriage. So, we moved in November of 1994, and I began working for Arthur Andersen LLP, at the time one of the "big five" global accounting firms. The extensive training, numerous clients, and a highly skilled staff made it a fast-paced and competitive environment. Shahram, using his training in the art of mold-making, worked on projects making decorative plaster moldings for newly constructed homes. He had given up on pursuing a career in petroleum engineering years earlier. The hostage-taking incident at the American embassy in Tehran had made it almost impossible for an Iranian to get a job in that field, and he needed to find a way to be productive.

I began attending a small church called The Iranian Community Church of Atlanta, where I spent a lot of time trying to understand the teachings of Christ, and how it could evolve my life. Little by little, I learned about the overall message of the Bible, the message of love, forgiveness, redemption, and reconciliation. I began understanding the stories in the Bible as not just something that happened in the past, but reflective of how we react today. The teachings of Christ about renewing our thinking had resonated powerfully with me, since the days of studying psychology in college. My world views were changing, and the questions of my mind and heart were being answered.

I was stunned to learn that God had entered our world and affected history! God was not just a distant spectator as I had assumed all my life. Absolute truth had revealed Himself to us! My heart was touched, heavens opened, I surrendered and was embraced by God's love. The father of the prodigal son is ready to accept His children with open arms when they come to Him.

A radical change began in me; a supernatural awakening took place. Suddenly, God had become a part of the equation, and now I was seeing His footprints everywhere and in everything. I no longer explained away events as coincidences but rather saw the hand of God in them. It was a fresh awareness of God's presence. Why hadn't I seen it before? Something had come alive in me! A part of my brain, dormant before, was awakened. A new sense, unlike sight, hearing, or touch, but an unseen sense, had been born. My colorless life became festive and joyful. The joy of knowing that the Creator of the universe was not standing on the sidelines detached, but was active in the lives of His creation. Christians believe that the spirit of Christ within us awakens our spirit, thus the term "born again." According to the Bible, I was dead and now I am alive!

One night I had a profound dream:

> In my dream I was lying on a bed. My sister Simin was kneeling on the floor beside me as I told her about my experience with God. I desperately wanted her to understand that the experiences

were real. Then, I heard a sound like the roaring of a train, and a book was opened and I looked. It was the book of Daniel, and I heard a voice saying in Farsi, Persian language "Man ghom e to ra nejat khaham dad" (translated: I will save your tribe.) The book abruptly closed, and I awakened from the dream.

It was some time past midnight, and I was now wide awake. My dream was exceptionally vivid, but I couldn't understand its meaning. I got up slowly, and quietly took my Bible and walked into the closet. I turned on the light and closed the door, so I wouldn't disturb my sleeping husband. I began searching and running my fingers through the contents of the Bible. I was ecstatic when I saw the book of Daniel listed in the contents. I knew Daniel was a prophet but I had no idea there was a book called Daniel in the Bible! I also discovered through later Bible studies that Daniel lived in exile in Persia for most of his life. Persia, an empire, which extended from India to Ethiopia, permitted the return of the Jews to Israel, 70 years after their exile by the Babylonians.[6] The Bible says a lot about Persia and the Persians.

But what did the dream mean and who was my tribe? In the Persian/English dictionary "ghom" is translated as tribe, people, and group of followers, or a nation. I began writing my dream and other spiritual experiences in a journal. Journaling had always been very healing for me. It allowed me to organize my thoughts and express my emotions. I still had my journals from high school tucked

---

[6]   The Persian king, Cyrus the Great, permitted the return of the Jews to Israel.

away in a box in the attic thinking that by keeping them, I could remain connected to my past.

❦ ❦ ❦

Shahram had become engrossed in Eastern philosophies. Buddhism, Hinduism, and Zoroastrianism intrigued his curious mind. He was not at all a religious man, yet was drawn to spirituality and open to the mystical. He considered Christianity a religion and he hated organized religion. I was busy going to various Bible studies and one night he went into a fit of rage when I came home from a particularly lengthy Bible study. He called me a fanatic, and grabbed my Bible and ripped it into pieces. My Farsi Bible, which I had meticulously marked and underlined, was now torn apart! I was heartbroken. I could not understand his rage. But soon thereafter, not out of a quest for the truth but in his curiosity, he began reading the Bible himself. He questioned, challenged, argued, and wrestled with many issues that puzzled him. The Bible, unlike the Muslim's general belief that the prophets were sinless, revealed the sins of the prophets and the disciples. Also, it contained amazing insight into the psychology of human nature, the spiritual warfare with the enemy within, and our negative thought patterns. A battle was raging within him. So he began studying the Bible vigorously. Some days he would spend most hours of the day studying. He finished reading the Bible in a few months. His thirst for spiritual consciousness was being quenched by the teachings of Christ.

Shahriar, an Iranian atheist, who had become a Christian and worship leader in my church, took him under his wing and attempted to answer his profound questions. However, Shahram remained a skeptic. Yet despite his resistance, he was finally tilted toward the truth of Christianity through a profound spiritual dream. Although I didn't believe that even God could change this incredibly strong-willed and skeptical man, I nevertheless asked Shahriar and a group of Christian friends to pray for him. One night he had a spiritual visitation that changed the course of his life!

> That night, he dreamt of being lost in those same treacherous mountains in Iran he had escaped from years before, the same place where the voice assured him that everything would be alright. In the dream, Christ appeared to him, saying, "Come, follow me." He awoke from the dream shaken up. He thought that perhaps he had too much to eat that night. He got up from our bed and went to the living room and fell asleep on the couch. He had exactly the same dream! He could not go back to sleep after the third dream in which Christ told him, "If you want to help your people, come and follow me."

Grieved by the adversities he had witnessed during his time in Iran, the secret yearning of his heart was to somehow, in some way, help his people. That morning he sheepishly told me about his dream. He said he didn't want me to think he was crazy. However, receiving an invitation from the King of the Universe, the Supreme Being, is not something to ignore. He had a momentous decision to make. Yet for him at that moment there were no reservations, he chose Christ. That Sunday in church, he publicly announced his newly found faith.

In November 1995, we had our annual retreat at a lodge called Fellowship Valley nestled in the North Georgia Mountains. It was surrounded by acres of woodlands with wooden cabins within walking distance of a lake. The conference room housed a small kitchen where we prepared and served our meals during our stay. Most Persians enjoy gourmet foods, and during mealtime the entire center was filled with the wonderful aromas of garlic, turmeric, and the sweet smell of saffron rice. There were walking trails to the other side of the lake where we held the baptism ceremony. The water in the lake was cold in November. Nevertheless, Shahram wanted to be baptized in the lake. We all lined up for the baptism at the water's edge. After prayer, Pastor Farhad immersed him in the lake water then brought him up, as a sign of new life. There was a lot of cheering and rejoicing from the crowd.

After the baptism, we dedicated a banner to the church. I had handcrafted a purple banner using fabric, beads, and bits of reflective glass, designed with a large silver cross in the center, a rising dove from the reflective glass, and the words Hope, Faith, and Love in Farsi. The banner represented the light of truth shining in the darkness. The celebration that night was festive as we gathered around a campfire near the lake, singing worship songs and dancing to the accordion played by Shahriar until hours past midnight.

🦋 🦋 🦋

I was a relatively new Christian; I felt alive, hopeful and was full of zeal, wanting to tell the whole world about my newly found faith. It puzzled me when people did not respond or seemed to be turned off by my approach. I expected everyone to understand exactly what I had experienced. My faith was real but not mature. My character and wisdom did not match my zeal, and often I appeared foolish. In seeking what I perceived as God's desire, I became a very busy bee!

Every morning at 6:30, my prayer partner, Noori, would call me to pray over the phone. We would begin by reading one of the Psalms, and pray for 20 minutes before I would get ready for work. It was a precious way to start the day. What connected us together was our love for God.

For most Iranians, every event is usually organized around food, and not just finger food, but gourmet Persian stews with exotic herbs and spices over saffron rice. So Friday nights were spent with a group of friends, hungry to know God, discussing and discovering the mysteries of the Bible over dinner. I was like a little kid who had been given a box of assorted chocolates, each containing a treasure to be discovered.

I began taking keyboard lessons with Valerie, the pianist of our church. Like learning a new language, I was taught the musical alphabets, chord progressions, time signature, and musical scales. Every afternoon when I arrived home from work, for a couple of hours I enjoyed practicing Iranian worship songs. In church during worship, I could sense the music seep slowly into my body, and the lyrics would bring tears to my eyes as I was being drawn closer and closer to God.

Soon I found myself on the worship team of a newly formed church called the Iranian Church of Hope, singing and playing the keyboard. With Pastor Sasan, his family and a few members, we began evangelizing among the Iranian people. We established outreach programs, retreats and Bible studies with Pastor Sasan as our teacher.

🦋 🦋 🦋

In 1997, I left my "perceived" secure job as a tax manager for Arthur Andersen to become self-employed in my area of expertise as a CPA. It turned out that my job at Arthur Anderson hadn't been so secure after all, because a few years after I left the firm, the century-old gigantic accounting firm was indicted by the Justice Department for its handling of Enron audits, which led to its demise.

My professional skills and experience had kept me marketable, so after leaving the firm, I was able to contract with United Parcel Service to work on special projects in their tax department. It was a timely and a welcome change from my fast-paced job at Arthur Andersen. By forming a corporation, I was able to contract with Coca-Cola Company and other major corporations to help them with their state tax compliance. This was a golden opportunity in my career. I was able to stay busy working all year and take some time off between contracts. This gave me more time to pursue my new passion. Worldly pleasures had lost their glamour, and I was now ready and eager to know and serve God.

After some time, Shahram became disappointed with church in general. Feeling it was not living up to his ideal of what Christianity should be, he did not attend church as often. He began focusing on the application of the spiritual disciplines taught in the Bible. Practicing the meditative and contemplative prayers, observing his negative thoughts, and seeking consciousness through Christ's teachings became his pastime. One verse in the Bible seemed to consume him. He would spend hours meditating on that verse. *"Be still and know that I am God."* Psalm 46:10. What he didn't know, was that he was being prepared for the trials ahead and for the testing of his life. There are times in our lives when the only thing we can do is abide in Him, be still, and know that He is God.

4

Storms of Life

*Sometimes, all we need for our pain to disappear
is a small voice of compassion in the distance.*

It was August 31, 1997. I was at the airport waiting for
the plane to take off from Houston, where I spent a few
days visiting my family. My sister Simin, who was now living
in Los Angeles, was also there. We had a wonderful time
together. The airport was busy; suddenly there was a lot of
commotion around the television. All eyes and ears were on
the screen. Everything came to a halt as they announced that
Princess Diana had died in a car crash! People were staring
at each other in disbelief. "How could this be?" A sense of
sadness engulfed me realizing that tragedy can strike in the
middle of the night, when all seems quiet.

I was back in Atlanta and back to the routine of everyday
life. On my way to work, I would often stop by a coffee
shop to buy my morning coffee, before venturing into the
Atlanta traffic. During the long drive to the office, I listened
to my favorite Christian radio station. Lately, I had been
catching an inspiring program by someone I only knew as
Joni.[7] I loved listening to her angelic voice, which inspired

---

[7] Joni Eareckson Tada, Joni and Friends Radio Program

me. Her messages were always profound and insightful. Sometimes I sat in my car in the parking lot and waited for her message to finish, before going into the office. I was shocked to discover that she was paralyzed! At the time, I had no idea how her testimony would affect my life.

One morning, as I was rushing around getting ready for work, I heard a gentle, quiet voice within me saying, *"I will never leave you nor forsake you."* It made me slow down and ponder. There comes a time in our lives when we have to pass through the fire and my time had come.

🦋　🦋　🦋

It was near the end of November 1997. I decorated our Christmas tree for the upcoming holidays, as my husband watched. He never got too excited about these traditions. December 1st was both my birthday and our wedding anniversary. Shahram decided to try his new recipe for duck. He didn't mind cooking as long as it was experimental, so we spent a quiet day at home and enjoyed a candlelight dinner that night. We slept in the guest bedroom since a professional artist was painting our bedroom ceiling to look like a blue sky with feathery and fluffy clouds. That was my birthday gift!

The day was December 3, 1997. On that cold, crisp morning, I put on my black suit with my favorite yellow sweater for work. I was a bit tired. Around 8:00 that morning, I grabbed my briefcase filled with client files and ran out of the house to the car, anxious to get an early start on the day. I turned the ignition and headed out of the driveway. As I approached the main road to leave our subdivision, my mind was planning out my day. I had several meetings to attend and would not be home until later in the evening.

What I didn't know, was that in a heartbeat my life would be forever altered! The difference between life as I had always known it, and a life of confusion and uncertainty, was just a matter of a few seconds. As soon as I made the left turn out of our subdivision, a sudden jerk immediately shook me as the thunderous crash of metal slamming into metal rattled the quiet morning. I did not see the other car approaching before it violently struck my car broadside. I didn't exactly know what had happened, but I realized that my head had dropped down to my chest. With all my strength I tried to sit up, but I couldn't move. I concentrated as hard as I could with all my willpower . . . but nothing happened. I just sat there in a stupor, not quite able to understand what was happening to me. I remember hearing voices, seeing faces looking down at me, asking me questions. In the confusion, everything became fuzzy. A paramedic, who just happened to be driving by on his way to work, helped me to breathe while waiting for an ambulance to arrive. Had he not been there, I doubt I would be here today and you wouldn't be reading this book.

A neighbor who had witnessed the crash called my husband. Shahram rushed to the scene of the accident. When he saw me, he knew it was serious. He said a short prayer. "God, you have allowed this to happen, so . . . you take care of us yourself."

I don't remember the ride in the ambulance as I was rushed to the nearest hospital. Shahram followed in his car. As medical staff carried me on a stretcher into the Emergency Room, the reality of the situation struck me with fear. In panic, I remember crying, "I'm broken," when I heard a sweet whisper in my ear, "Yes, but your spirit is not broken." Those comforting words of encouragement were from one of the nurses. Her words enabled me to calm down and brought me back to the reality that God was still in control.

Feeling lost and confused, I tried to unravel where I was, and why I was there. I was x-rayed over and over, and later brought to an examination room where doctors and nurses hovered over me. The drugs I was given put my mind in a haze. I don't remember much of what happened next. One of my first memories in the hospital is lying on a hospital bed that seemed to be rocking from side to side, and seeing my husband's face hovering over me. I struggled to speak, and in a whisper I said, "I want to die." I felt just awful, utterly sick, and totally devastated.

Doctors gave the verdict, a broken neck at C-5 (5ᵗʰ cervical vertebrae), which caused a severed spinal cord and complete paralysis from the shoulders down. At that time, I did not know exactly all that quadriplegia entailed, and I was too numb to hear or understand what the doctors were telling us. I closed my eyes, wishing it was all just a bad dream, and yet I knew I had no control over the circumstances in which I now found myself.

Surgery was scheduled immediately. The doctors fused the bones in my neck during surgery, using plates, screws and part of my hipbone. After the surgery, hooked up to all kinds of tubes and machines, I looked like something out of a science-fiction movie. I was in a halo, a metallic ring that was screwed into my skull to immobilize my neck and prevent movement. Metal braces that extended from padded shoulders supported the metallic ring. A respirator pumped air in and out of my lungs. Lying on the bed, I could not do anything but stare at the white ceiling with my arms at my sides. Unable to turn my head, I couldn't even tell what the room looked like.

My family immediately flew in from Houston to be with me. It was very devastating for them to see me suffer, and I could sense their despair. My sister Fari stayed with me day and night during the most critical days in the hospital. I desperately needed her gentle and warm presence. She would cover me with a blanket when I was cold or wipe my sweat when I was hot. I felt hopeful with my family around me.

Within days after the surgery, they transferred me to the Shepherd Center in Atlanta. It was a rehabilitation center for brain and spinal-cord-injury patients to recover from their injury and to learn a new way of life. It was close to Christmastime. The images of warm houses, decorated Christmas trees, candles, and the sweet smell of cookies were replaced with a desolate room with no windows, no blue sky, no sunshine, no trees, just somber emptiness. Suddenly, I had been cut off from the world.

Nurses came in to turn me over, feed me, change my bandages, and give me more medication. Whatever else they were doing, I didn't dare to ask. I moved in and out of consciousness, disoriented, never knowing the time of day or the day of the week. I couldn't feel my own body; it seemed to belong to someone else! The metallic taste in my mouth from all of the medications was turning my stomach. My body could no longer control its temperature; I was either sweating or shivering, feeling miserable and out of control. Waves of panic rushed over me as I faced the harsh reality that I could no longer trust my body to do what it needed.

🦋 🦋 🦋

During those long days in the hospital, my soul hungered for a loving touch, a prayer, or just family and friends to be there, and I was surrounded by love. Most of the time, I wasn't alone. My family drove back and forth from Houston every weekend to see me. Our friends, our church community, my coworkers, and other relatives from different parts of the country came to comfort me. After hearing about my accident, Pastor Ramin, from the Valley Iranian Church in California, along with his assistant, flew in specifically to pray for me. I had so many visitors every day that the hospital staff was baffled. I felt an overwhelming love from all the visitors. They brought gifts, food, prayers and loving hearts.

I remember one day asking my husband for a cuddly teddy bear to keep me company. I felt like a baby who needed her security blanket. Soon I was surrounded by all kinds of bears. My friends brought all sorts of adorable, fluffy, hug-able bears: angel bears, Coca-Cola polar bears, a honey bear and even a huge papa bear. Besides gifts, visitors also brought food. Our friends brought so much Persian food that the aroma of turmeric and saffron hit your nostrils as soon as you walked off the elevator to the hospital floor. My room was always filled with flowers and countless cards of encouragement. I have lasting memories of people's kindness and generosity. Through their unconditional love, I found the strength to go on and fight for my life.

I spent the Christmas holidays in the hospital. Nights were lonely. I remember one particular night lying in bed, in my halo, staring at the white ceiling. That night Shahram stayed with me. Suddenly we heard the pleas of a woman in another room, apparently in great pain. Her pleas were continuous and became more piercing as the night closed in. "Lord, have mercy on me," she kept repeating over and over. Behind every door of this corridor was a distinct story. I didn't know her saga, but I longed to somehow comfort her. I wanted to hold her hand and ease her pain, but I was helpless to do anything for myself, let alone her.

Suddenly, a sweet melody began to form in my mind, a certain tune to the rhythm of her plea. I began to sing out loud with the melody, "Lord, have mercy on her, Lord, have mercy on her." Shahram and I began singing and the louder we sang, the quieter she became. We sang until her groaning disappeared and she fell asleep! Sometimes, all we need for our pain to disappear is a small voice of compassion in the distance.

🦋 🦋 🦋

One day, a visitor entered my room. I recognized her face, but I couldn't remember her name. In her soft and gentle voice she whispered in my ear, "You don't know me, but I've heard about you during our prayers in church, and I've come to help you. What can I do for you? Would you like me to wash your hair?" she asked. It felt like my hair had not been washed in months. My scalp was constantly itching. Since the doctors had removed the metallic halo around my head, my hair could now be washed. Oh, how I wanted my hair to be washed. She had sensed my need! I was ecstatic. Her name was Yvonne. She had to search around the hospital floor for all the necessary materials, and the nurses were not very cooperative. Finally, she was able to collect everything she needed to shampoo my hair. The sense of warm water and the gentle strokes of her hands on my head were refreshing to my soul. She discovered a pressure sore on the back of my head and notified the nurses, and they contacted the doctors immediately. The unconditional love of Christ, manifested through Yvonne, washed much more than just my hair. She washed away my pains.

In about a month after the initial surgery, my health turned for the worst. I had pain, fever, and difficulty swallowing. I also noticed an unpleasant odor in the room. An x-ray revealed a massive infection in my neck, which later was determined to be caused by a hole in my esophagus. The foul odor I smelled was from the infection in my neck! I remember clearly the doctor looking at the stitches saying, "This is not good!" As he was explaining to my family the procedures for recovery from the wound, I wanted to run away. It was as if he was talking about a machine that needed a few screws and bolts changed; "Surgery to remove the plates, put a tube in her neck to suction the saliva, another tube in her stomach for feeding." I was petrified. It was just more than I could bear.

They needed to remove the infection immediately. Surgery was scheduled for the following day. Since Shepherd Center was not equipped for surgeries, all surgeries had to be performed at Piedmont Hospital located next door to the center. They had to wheel me on a stretcher through a long underground tunnel to get to Piedmont Hospital. As they transferred me on a gurney to surgery, staring at the ceiling, the huge paintings of colorful butterflies that seemed to be dancing all around me captured my attention. Parts of the underground tunnel had cobblestone flooring, so my body would shake with every move of the wheels across the floor. In my stupor, the whole thing seemed comical, like a scene from a Marx Brothers movie.

After the second surgery, I was once again in a metallic halo! In order for the perforated esophagus to heal, I was not allowed to eat or drink for weeks, and was fed through a tube in my stomach, and was intravenously receiving massive doses of antibiotics. Another tube was inserted in the area of the perforated esophagus to suction all fluids and keep it dry. My mouth had become as dry as a cotton ball, and the only way I was allowed to relieve the dryness was to have someone swirl a wet swab around the inside of my mouth.

Being paralyzed, unable to do anything for myself, I had to communicate my every need to others. With the tubes in my throat, I was now prevented from speaking. The only way I could communicate was to spell a word by blinking twice, to choose the correct letter of the alphabet as someone pointed to the letters on a sheet. It was very frustrating, and often the person couldn't understand me because of a wrong letter or improper spacing between words. My eyes tired easily and began to burn after a few words. Discouraged, I often retreated to my loneliness.

I had grown frail from losing so much weight. The doctors didn't think I could survive the infection. Because of lack of movement, my muscles were atrophying before my eyes. I was frightened the first time my sister-in-law Kathy held up a mirror so I could see myself. There were agonizing days of suffering when I did not think I could bear another moment. My mind was racing with questions, "What is happening to me? What would my new life be like? What would be my future?"

Friends kept quoting Romans 8:28 "*And we know that in all things God works for the good of those who love him, who have been called according to his purpose.*" "But how could anything good come out of this? Why has this happened to me?" I thought. In my despair, the only hope seemed to be a miraculous healing. "God must be up to something big!" I thought. "After all, the only way most Iranians would come to believe that Jesus is the Savior would be to witness a miracle." I kept hoping for a miracle, and that hope helped me to hang on to life.

☙ ☙ ☙

I had become extremely dependent on my husband. I desperately needed to see his familiar face and to sense his familiar touch. My soul craved for someone who could understand, and he was a constant source of hope to me. Being so engrossed in my own predicament, I was totally oblivious to what he was going through. His life had suddenly turned upside down as well. He was numb from exhaustion after spending much of his time in the hospital. He desperately needed to maintain his courage and determination to go on. He knew that recovery from this would not come quickly but would be more like running a marathon.

He wrote this poem in Farsi during those dark days in the hospital: (translated)

> In our desperation,
> when the depth of darkness sees no end,
> and death casts its shadow on our days,
> while pain besieges our souls,
> our only hope in hopelessness
> is the merciful and forgiving God.
> He illuminates our path,
> and enlightens our hearts.
>
> Dear God,
> help us;
> grant us strength and endurance,
> so in the midst of our suffering and despair,

we glorify you.

Amen
February 13, 1998

It was late one night when Shahram decided to drive home after spending a long day in the hospital. I had asked the nurses for more pain medication, and I was in a daze from the drugs. After I fell asleep, he sneaked out of the room and headed towards the parking lot.

It was a moonless night and the stars seemed to have lost their shimmer. The exhaustion from spending all day in the hospital had weighed him down. A heavy sadness that had lingered since the day of the accident engulfed him. His days had lost their color, followed by nights of restless sleep.

By the time he got home, it was raining. Once home, he lay down on the sofa, where he had been spending much of his time when he was not at the hospital. Before he could fall asleep, he heard a rhythmic ticking sound coming from the kitchen. He crawled off the sofa and headed towards the sound. To his horror, he discovered that the kitchen roof was leaking! Worn out and feeling defeated, he yelled in anger, "What else can go wrong?" He grabbed a towel and a bucket, and placed it under the spot where the water was leaking from the kitchen roof. He decided he wasn't going to worry about that now, he was exhausted.

Shahram crawled back onto the sofa. As his eyelids began to feel the heaviness of sleep, he was haunted by an image. He could see my face, calling him. He didn't know if he was hallucinating, but the image would not fade from his consciousness. It stole his sleep and in despair, compelled him to drive back to the hospital.

Once he entered the room, he saw my breathing was very shallow. My face appeared pale, almost blue. He called the nurses, who immediately rushed me to the Emergency Room. My lungs had filled with fluid, and I was close to suffocation!

I was in the critical care unit once again, before being transferred to recovery. With my level of spinal cord injury, I did not have control of my diaphragm, so several times a day the nurses would huddle over me and help me to cough. One nurse would press upward with both hands on my diaphragm while another nurse, using a tube, suctioned the fluid from my lungs. That was a dreadful experience, which never became easier.

🦋   🦋   🦋

Most of my time at Shepherd was spent going from surgery to recovery room, and back to surgery. My body continued to weaken; my health was deteriorating, and due to other complications more surgeries were needed. "Whatever can go wrong will go wrong." Murphy's Law was not my favorite motto; however, I now couldn't help but think that in my case, it was true. I felt locked inside a body that was failing. "It wasn't supposed to be this way!" I thought.

In times of our greatest need, God's love and encouragement is manifested in many ways. One day when I was alone in my room, a woman appeared at the foot of my bed. She seemed to be in her early 50s, dressed professionally in a suit, with her hair neatly pulled back. She gracefully leaned over my bed, tenderly looked into my eyes and asked if she could pray for me. The only words I could utter were, "Yes, please." She began to pray ever so softly, ever so gently and ever so beautifully. Her voice was soothing, as if an angel was worshipping God to music in my room! My pain was eased with every word, and all my cares seemed to dissipate. Her prayer embraced me with a peace I had never experienced before, and I fell into a much-needed restful sleep.

I don't know how long I slept, but I felt refreshed when I awoke. She was gone. I asked the nurses who she was, and they said they didn't know anything about her. I thought maybe she was the Chaplain, but I remembered having met the Chaplain. I desperately needed the peace her prayer brought. She had the answers to the deepest longing in my heart, and I pleaded with God to send her back. And then one day, she came again! When I saw her, I wanted to ask her all kinds of questions, but I couldn't utter a word. I was enchanted and speechless. Immediately, I felt the same peace as she began to pray. I fell into a deep sleep and did not get a chance to talk to her at all. That was the last time I ever saw her. Could she have been an angel who was sent to comfort me?

🦋 🦋 🦋

As I recovered from the perforated esophagus and gained more strength, they transferred me to a wheelchair for an hour or two a day. This would prevent pressure sores and would allow me to get used to sitting up. Being lifted into a wheelchair petrified me and made me dizzy. It seems ridiculous now, but not having control of my body was a new and terrifying experience. The only way I can describe it is the feeling you have on a roller coaster, with minimal security holding you in the seat and dropping down a steep hill!

I thought I was making progress and that the difficult days were over, when suddenly I suffered an excruciating headache, with no relief, even with the strongest pain medication. Any sound or light hurt me like a sharp blow. Two days later, I was going back to surgery for placement of a shunt in my head, to reduce the buildup of the spinal fluid around my brain and spine, which was causing the headaches.

Lying there on my back, helpless and exposed, staring at the white ceiling all day, I found myself pondering things I had not taken time to consider before. With everything stripped away, I began to see the futility of relying on myself, the frailty of life, and the vanity of accomplishments I held dear. For the first time in my life, I realized that I really needed God.

5

The Vision

"Never will I leave you; never will I forsake you."
Hebrews 13:5

I tried to hold up and win the fight, but one day I broke down in tears. Feelings of self-pity overpowered me, and I sobbed continuously and uncontrollably. The thought of being confined to a wheelchair and not even able to use my hands was devastating to me. I didn't want to become a burden. Unable to see where my life was going, I only saw the negative, and everything seemed dark. One thought was ever-present: life as I had known it was finished. "What is going to make this life worth living?" I thought. I refused to allow the doctors to perform any more surgeries. Depression had set in, and at times suicide seemed like the only possible means of escaping my reality. The psychiatrist placed me on anti-depressants, which I took for one year after the accident.

My dreams shattered, I was questioning "But . . . where is God?" Unable to do anything for myself, I often asked my husband to read to me from the Bible's book of Job. I wanted to find God's answer to Job regarding his suffering. I needed some answers! To my dismay, I never found the answer for Job's suffering. His conclusion to his predicament seemed to say, "I thought I knew You, but now I have seen You." The suffering brought him closer to God, and now he had an even better understanding of who God was. "Is that what I needed?" I thought.

I was haunted by the same lingering thought: "Where is God in all of this?" But the heavens were silent. "Does He even care? If He really cares, why am I getting worse instead of better?" I would plead with God to draw near and to provide His abiding presence, to no avail. I felt abandoned by the God I had come to know and love. Alone in my room, I found myself wondering whether my beliefs were true after all. "Was Jesus for real?" I questioned.

And then one morning, when I opened my eyes, I noticed a crumpled piece of paper on the counter across from my hospital bed. As I focused, I saw an image, an origami of what appeared to be a figure. It was an amazing image of Jesus Christ, carrying someone in His arms whom I perceived to be me. The heavy weight of my lifeless body was in the loving arms of the Holy One, as He tenderly gazed upon me.

Whoever had crumpled that piece of paper could not have known by whom his fingers were being directed! Who could have folded a sheet of paper so precisely, so meticulously and masterfully as to produce the shape I was witnessing? No one but the invisible hand of God Himself. I felt the abiding presence of God whispering, "*I am here, I am with you, I am carrying you.*" That image became my assurance that God was there, and He had indeed been carrying me. When my husband walked into the room, he too, saw the same image! God had answered my fervent pleas, with an image that contained a world of meaning. My God had not deserted me!

God's presence was there all along, but I couldn't see Him in the darkness of my despair. His presence was in the smile of each person who came to visit, in the warm touch of a friend's hand, and in the love and compassion I received from others. Years later, I realized that when we are in the valley of despair, when life doesn't make sense and we feel abandoned and alone, we must hang on to the promises of God.

He promises,
>   *"Never will I leave you; never will I forsake you."*
>   Hebrews 13:5.

He promises,
>   *"For I know the plans I have for you," declares the LORD, "plans to prosper you and not to harm you, plans to give you hope and a future."*
>   Jeremiah 29:11.

YES, God has a plan and a purpose for my life no matter what it looks like now.

>   *"I can do all this through him who gives me strength."*
>   Philippians 4:13.

YES, no matter what happens, God will give me the strength to handle it.

If we learn to walk with God when there is still light, we won't have to search for Him when we are in the dark. Life can be empty, bleak and hopeless without faith in God. Slowly, I discovered a fierce power within me to battle and to not give up. There was a glimpse of hope; I wanted to get well, to overcome, to live, to dream again, and that was the turning point. It took a spiritual battle for me to fight for my life.

♥ ♥ ♥

It was now near springtime. On a sunny day, I had a much-welcomed visit from Pastor Sasan and his family. I was finally able to sit longer in a wheelchair, and they sneaked me out of the hospital to a surprise party of friends at a nearby pizza place. It was such a joy to get out of that hospital for a few hours. That was the day I discovered why I loved pizza so much. It is the joy of grabbing a hot slice with my fingers, melted cheese stretching at its sides, bringing it to my mouth, and devouring it. That feeling cannot compare to someone else slicing it with a knife, placing a small bite on a fork, and feeding it to me. By the time it reached my mouth, well, it was cold! And that's when pizza lost its position as one of my favorite foods. I was beginning to learn that joy had to be rediscovered and redefined. What previously brought joy was now a nuisance.

Sundays were especially lonely. I missed going to church, participating in worship, and being among my friends. When we moved to Georgia, I was homesick for my family, and the friends I had made at church filled that void. They truly became family to me. My heart longed to be with them, so our friend Shahriar, the worship leader at our church, brought the church into my lonely hospital room! He called me from a speaker phone at the church before the start of worship on Sunday mornings. He placed the speaker phone on the stage, where he led the worship followed by the sermons, so I could listen live to each Sunday service.

There were also many moments of laughter and joy. One day, Shahriar and my husband played backgammon in my room by placing a soft leather board on my stomach. Each of them sat on opposite sides of my bed and got me excited in the heat of this game of much commotion, boasting, and wit. If you haven't seen two Iranians play backgammon, you don't know what this game is all about!

Incidentally, most of the nurses caring for me were Christians. Some would pray for me or sing to me when they saw me distressed. They were God's instruments of healing. And of course there were a few who didn't really belong in the field.

Looking back, I don't view my experience in the hospital as only a sad juncture, but as very much a spiritual journey. In the midst of suffering, the Holy Spirit was near, providing a supernatural strength and peace to help us persevere. God's enduring presence touched others also. I have a message book, given to me in the hospital by my friend, Caroline. My visitors would leave me messages when I was either asleep or busy with the nurses, so that my husband could later read them to me. It has become a treasure for me. This is a part of what our friend Shahriar wrote one day, translated:

> "If I had gone to sleep on December 3rd and had awakened in this hospital room, seeing Nasrin laying here with motionless legs and arms at her sides, her head shaved, metal staples that appear as if her head has been sown to her neck, hooked up to these machines, God knows after how many surgeries, six or seven perhaps, I would have thought this to be the most horrific nightmare ever!

But I didn't go to sleep on December 3rd and this is not a nightmare. Reality is sometimes more fearsome than we can imagine. I have no doubt that without the mercy of God we would not be able to face the nightmares of the realities of this world.

Yet despite the harsh appearances, in this place there is a spirit of peace, love and trust. I see a smile on Nasrin's face, and praise and worship on her lips. I see a new commitment from Shahram to run this Marathon. There is a life-giving power here that changes even the lives of those who have come to visit. The light of God is in this place!

Praise the Lord,
Shahriar"

My husband was a constant source of hope to me. Even under the most difficult circumstances, he could still make me laugh. He always makes light of things, even in the middle of our calamity. His humor helped me to find delight and experience joy, and it was healing to my soul. I remember one day he said, "You know what, honey? We don't have to worry about finding a great parking spot ever again!"

"Yeah . . . you're right!" I replied. At that, we both burst into laughter until we cried.

Shahram had befriended many of the patients and their families. He was uncommonly transparent, and they felt extremely at ease with him. A Korean woman was recovering from her injury in the room next to mine. I found out later that she and her husband were the owners of a store in town. She was a pharmacist and one morning decided to open the store by herself, when two gunmen stormed in, shot her, and took the money from the cash register. The injury left her paralyzed. I had not personally met her but had heard she was severely depressed. I told her husband that after my next scheduled surgery, I would try to talk to her and encourage her. I had discovered a divine strength and compassion to reach out to others, despite my own despondency.

Shahram spent hours talking to the Korean woman's husband. Conversations were deep and unusually candid. Their lives were woven together by the common pain they shared. They talked about ways to cope with the tragedy that had befallen them. Their discussions always steered towards the divine. He confided to my husband about struggling with thoughts of suicide. He said his life appeared meaningless and his future seemed bleak. He couldn't understand our peace in the midst of our adversity. He couldn't explain the hope he had seen in me, even though I was physically in much worse shape than his wife.

One night, while walking in the moonlight outside the hospital and smoking a cigarette, he asked my husband curiously, "What's going on here? Who are you people?"

Shahram replied, "Let me ask you a question. Are you a Buddhist?"

"Yeah," he answered, as he puffed his cigarette.

"Do you practice Zen? Do you meditate?" Shahram asked.

He frowned. "No, I never had time for that kind of stuff."

"Well, since you asked for the reason for my hope, I'll tell you. We are Christians. We believe in Jesus Christ as our Lord and our savior."

His voice rose. "Oh, I don't believe that stuff."

"You asked me, why we are the way we are, and I'm telling you that the reason is the Holy Spirit."

"What's the Holy Spirit?" he asked condescendingly.

"It is the Spirit of God within us, in our hearts, that enables us to have peace, in spite of our suffering. He gives us hope that is beyond our circumstances and understanding."

"I don't believe that stuff," he said bluntly, as he ground his cigarette under his shoe.

Shahram looked at him intently and said, "I'm not asking you to believe it or not. I'm just telling you, that's why we are the way we are."

After a long silence, bitter tears streaming down his cheeks, he broke down and told Shahram, "I don't know how to go on. I don't know what to do."

They stood there for some time and talked. Shahram put his hand on his shoulder and said quietly, "Look, you have no choice but to rely on God for meeting your needs and for giving you the strength to go on."

As they parted, while walking back to the building, my husband heard a voice in the distance crying out loud, "I have . . . no choice . . . , I have no choice."

Sometimes, it is only in our brokenness, on our knees, that we are willing to look into our hearts to find that God had been waiting there all along. Pastor Ramin, who was visiting me from California, prayed for the Korean couple and introduced the husband to a Korean church in town where they could get spiritual healing and much needed community support. That Sunday, after visiting his wife in the hospital, he and his children were off to church.

6

Footprints of God

Inner freedom is real freedom

After I had recovered enough to sit in a wheelchair for longer periods, the nurses would wheel me to the "garden." It was a green space outdoors specially designed for patients to learn the art of gardening. Here you could find raised gardens with all sorts of flowers planted in them. Shrubbery surrounded the walkways and oak trees provided shade from the sun. There was a fountain at a corner of the garden, which enhanced the landscape and where birds wet their feathers.

On a warm spring day, after recovery from my last surgery, I was in a wheelchair in the garden. My hair was shaved to allow placement of a shunt to release excess fluid around my brain and spine, which had caused my excruciating headaches. The stitches extended from the top of my scalp to one side of my neck. When seen from above, they formed the shape of a big question mark on my bald head.

I wheeled my power chair to a secluded spot in the garden. I was in a grave mood that day. I wanted to be free, to escape from this reality and to fly to a far, far away land.

Suddenly my eyes caught a glimpse of a butterfly on the ground beside my wheelchair! As I looked closer, I noticed there were three butterflies resting on the ground, gracefully flapping their delicate wings. My thoughts shifted to the splendor of the scene. The brilliant array of colors, royal blues and shiny black with gold spots embellished their fragile wings. They just rested on a patch of dirt, gently flapping their wings! I became engrossed in watching their every delicate movement.

It seemed the progressive movement of time had stopped. I don't know how long it was before they thrust their wings forward and one by one began to fly. They turned around to face me as if inviting me to come. Their erratic, yet graceful flight became a delicate gliding as they soared into the air.

Suddenly, I was there,
flying among them.
I could hear their song and sense their joy,
as we flew swiftly toward the horizon.
I was dancing with butterflies!
With the cool and crisp air breezing in my face,
I turned my head to look behind me.
There at a distance,
on the ground below,
I saw a set of footprints,
beside the woman in the wheelchair,
as she gazed up into the sky,
watching the dance of the butterflies.

That day I realized that inner freedom is real freedom, and I'll never be free unless my inner thoughts are free!

7

Coming Home

This was going to be a marathon, and not a sprint.

Most of my time at Shepherd was spent shuttling back and forth to surgery, so rehabilitation was limited to the last two or three weeks of my stay. The therapists poked me to see if there was any feeling left in my fingers. "Can you feel this?" "Can you feel that?" Mostly what I felt was an unpleasant feeling of needles and pins in my fingers. They were excited to discover some movement in my wrists because it meant with exercise over time, I would be strong enough to do many things using a hand cuff. So they began teaching me how to use different hand braces to do some of the most basic tasks in everyday life, such as eating, brushing my teeth, or writing. I didn't master any of them.

I remember being envious of the paraplegics because they could use their hands! During rehab they attempted to prepare us for life outside the hospital by showing many hours of videos and hands-on experiences. My family members also participated in training of caring for me. I was apprehensive about going home. Being in the hospital for months, it had become my new home where nurses were available, and where I knew I would be taken care of. My biggest fear was, having to depend on my husband for my care. Would this man who had never had the responsibility of caring for anyone, be able to take care of me now?

After four months, six surgeries, and some training, I was allowed to go home. The nurses helped to place me in the front seat of our car. Leaving the hospital, I noticed curb ramps in the vicinity of building entrances and on the streets. During the training at Shepherd Center, I was informed that the American's view of people with disabilities has been profoundly changed by the Americans with Disabilities Act (ADA)[8]. It has helped to create a society where easier access to public places is common, via curb cuts, ramps, lifts on buses, and other access designs. (Opportunities for the physically challenged offered in America are tremendous, and I am grateful for that.)

The drive home was not very long. As we came closer to our house, a deep sense of loneliness engulfed me, knowing that we were now totally on our own. When we reached our house, a semi-truck pulled into our driveway. The electric wheelchair I ordered had arrived! I was surprised that it was ready so soon, since we were told it would not be ready, until days after my arrival home. We had a step by the front door entrance and with the help of the driver, my husband was able to get me inside the house. Later, Fred, a friend from church helped us to build a ramp for the front entrance so I could have easy access with my wheelchair.

I had almost forgotten exactly what my house looked like! The daffodil bulbs we had planted were now blossoming bright yellow. The Christmas tree I had decorated before

---

[8] The ADA prohibits discrimination on the basis of disability in public accommodations, commercial facilities, transportation, telecommunications, employment, and State and local government,

the accident was still up, but it was now early spring. The mountains of mail on the dining room table spoke of the difficult and lonely months my husband must have endured.

It felt so strange riding around the house in a wheelchair, and it took some time to adjust. Since all the bedrooms were upstairs, we had to turn the downstairs living room into my bedroom. The painting of our bedroom ceiling to look like a blue sky with clouds, was completed while I was in the hospital, but I couldn't go upstairs to see it. There was no shower downstairs, and later my brother and sister-in-law helped us to build an accessible shower.

Soon after my arrival home, I was confronted with the reality of being totally dependent. It seemed like everything that brought joy was taken away from me. I felt nostalgic for the life I had taken for granted. I missed using my fingers, driving a car, sleeping in my own bedroom upstairs; I even missed doing the laundry! Life seemed like one endless program after another. There was bowel program, bladder control program, range of motion program . . . My world had stopped its fast pace, and now I had to be patient for everything. What was once so easy had become an impossible task. I experienced a lifetime of emotions in all its intensity, in just a few days. Sometimes, my frustrations would turn to anger, and anger would then turn to feelings of sorrow and despair. I realized, as my husband said early on, that this was going to be a marathon, and not a sprint.

Suddenly, I had become an observer rather than a participant in life. As I saw others around me preparing meals, and cleaning up, I just sat there nervously watching. Struggling to find my role and identity in this new life, I tried to disconnect myself from my past. Every picture that reminded me of the past was taken off the wall. "The sooner I accept my new self and my circumstances, the better off I will be!" So, I thought. I was never the type of person who dwelt in the past, but now without my past I felt hollow, empty, and lost.

There were signs of recurring depression. Thinking I will never be able to enjoy life again or laugh carelessly again. Activities and friends did not interest me. Assuming that nothing would ever get better, and there was nothing I could do to improve my situation, I sometimes felt hopeless, helpless and lifeless. Not knowing how to ask for help, or perhaps not even recognizing it as depression, I retreated into my loneliness.

For a while, Shahram cared for me all by himself. It was then that I realized men are not nurturers by nature. I also discovered that men, unlike women, tend to exclusively focus on doing one task at a time, and for him, sitting on the couch while waiting for the laundry to dry was considered a task! He did not want to hear about details and liked to speak in short phrases. It was best not to use my hinting language when I wanted something because he preferred direct but not bossy communication. And most importantly, he had no clue as to how to dress a woman. Most of the time he dressed me like a clown.

"Honey, this flowery shirt you dressed me in doesn't go with this plaid skirt," I would tell him.

"Ah . . . don't worry, you look just fine," was his reply.

Nevertheless, I was totally oblivious to the effects that care-giving can have on a person. Family caregivers, while feeling love, compassion and kindness may also feel overwhelmed, isolated, fatigued, anxious, guilty or depressed. The stress of the past months had taken its toll on Shahram. The bags under his eyes and added silver in his hair showed how deeply he had been affected. All attention was on me, and no one had acknowledged his feelings.

Through research over the years, I realized that many exhausted caregivers do not seek help because they do not even realize they have a recognizable condition known as "Caregiver Syndrome." They often don't know how to ask for help or feel guilty about it. Family caregivers must find a balance between their own needs and the needs of their loved ones. Getting a break, and having the time and opportunity to pamper themselves, are necessities for family caregivers.

After days of caring for me, he was overwhelmed and totally exhausted, and I was in tears. As if this wasn't enough, one day he got food poisoning. He did not tell me so that I wouldn't worry. He was vomiting upstairs and feeding and changing me downstairs. He was in utter despair, when "she" called!

She was a private nurse who occasionally visited the art room in the hospital. During one visit, she overheard two nurses talking about my husband's expertise in the art of mold making. She inquired where my room was and came up to visit. On the day we were packing our bags to leave the hospital, she walked in. She was a tall and thin African American woman in her early thirties. She wanted to learn everything about mold making and agreed to barter with us for her nursing services. We could not afford to hire a nurse, and here she was offering her services for free, just as we were leaving the hospital!

She was a huge help to us for those critical early days at home. Seeing how exhausted Shahram was, she even stayed some nights to help turn me over at night. Later, she confided in us that she was a recently recovered drug addict. After a car accident that almost took her life, she had accepted Christ. Our conversion story strengthened her fragile faith. As we prayed together, we thanked God for connecting our lives.

❦ ❦ ❦

We were practically broke. The financial hardships after a medical catastrophe are enormous. The changes needed to make our home accessible, plus the medical and home health care costs were overwhelming. Looking back, I can only say that with the grace of God, we were able to make it. Many of our family and friends, specifically two families in our church, helped to support us financially. We would not have been able to make it without their help. They truly demonstrated compassion, kindness, and friendship. We were humbly amazed and overcome with gratitude. With their help, we were able to install an accessible shower, purchase an accessible van, and make the necessary modifications to the house.

Since I had become self-employed prior to the accident, we had to purchase health insurance on our own. Ironically, we finally decided to purchase health insurance just a few months prior to the accident, when an insurance agent in our church approached us about it! We signed the insurance papers over dinner one night at our house. They covered most of my hospital bills, which were close to a million dollars. Our battle with the insurance company was triumphant in that we were eventually able to purchase an electric lift and a hospital bed. Still, I hated having my lovely home looking as cold and impersonal as a hospital.

Soon after coming home, I decided to visit my coworkers. It was good to see everyone, and I was told I could go back to work whenever I felt ready. It was a sweet proposition that helped to boost my ego, but I knew I would not be ready for some time. Rob, who had visited me quite often in the hospital and during my stay had kept everyone at work informed of my condition, was getting married and invited us to his wedding. He mentioned that my accident, like a wakeup call, had forever changed his life!

On Easter Sunday, with Pastor Sasan's encouragement, I went to church for the first time since the accident, to give a short testimony in front of our congregation. There were so many visitors that day. I did not know many of them, and was a bit nervous about being around so many people. The church seemed different than I remembered it, except for the familiar purple banner I had made years ago, which was still hanging on the wall. I felt all eyes were upon me, as I wheeled to the front of the stage and began speaking. My tension eased while I gave a short testimony. Afterwards, people gathered around me to offer comfort and I felt engulfed with the sweetest love.

Soon I began attending church regularly, and Shahriar bought me a xylophone, so I could play in church. He and his wife were such encouragers to me. I have fond memories of us, before the car accident, spending many evenings gathered around the piano at their house, singing worship songs. An engineer by profession, Shahriar was also a gifted musician and songwriter. He and my husband have written many Persian worship songs that have become some of the greatest songs that have been sung in our church. Often, Shahriar would find lyrics to a song by reading the Scripture and putting music to the words. Shahram would write memorable and catchy songs that would set a hook in the listener's mind.

I longed to revert to my familiar ways in life, and one way was to be able to participate in the church worship team again. So, I attempted to learn to play the xylophone

Shahriar gave me. But, I found it difficult to play with hand braces. My arms just weren't strong enough. In anger, I gave up and cried out to God, "Why did you send me to learn keyboard, when you knew I wouldn't be able to play for long?" It was just a cry of the heart, and I didn't expect an answer. Nevertheless, I heard an inner voice telling me "What makes you think I sent you there to learn to play?" I knew the voice! He never gave me the answers, but like a good counselor led me to search deep within for the answers.

I recalled my conversations before each lesson with Valerie, my keyboard teacher. She spoke of an unseen world, a spiritual world, of things I had not heard being discussed in our church before. She helped clarify my vague understanding of spiritual realities, and emphasized the importance of communicating with God every day, so that I would recognize His voice among the many voices that exist in the world. I felt safe discussing my dreams and my supernatural experiences with her.

For spiritually alive persons, there are many supernatural gifts and experiences from the Holy Spirit, such as visions, dreams, words of knowledge and prophecy. She also helped me to understand that demonic forces exist in our world, dwelling in the dark places in our hearts and minds that have not yet been transformed by the light of God. Valerie had been one of my spiritual teachers, without either of us realizing it!

ꟿ ꟿ ꟿ

Being paralyzed, unable to do many of the things that used to keep me busy, I found a lot of time to think, to question, to meditate and to read. I had so many unanswered questions: "Why didn't God prevent my accident? Was it predestined, or just my bad luck? Is there a purpose behind everything? Why does evil exist? Why do children die of starvation in Africa? Would somebody please tell me: Why is there so much suffering in this world?" My anger ultimately turned towards God, and I blamed Him for my accident.

As a young Christian, in my way of thinking, believing in God as my shield and protector translated into being immune from suffering. After all, I was now a child of God, and therefore under His umbrella of protection. I paid little attention to the words of Jesus saying, "In this world there will be troubles . . . !" But when life as I had known it suddenly changed, some things no longer made sense.

Some well-meaning friends tried to explain my injury as just a random event. "Life is a game of cards," they said. "You have to play the hand you are dealt." Some other people said it was a punishment from God for changing my religion from Islam, (changing one's religion from Islam is a crime punishable by death in the Islamic Republic of Iran.) However, I desperately needed to know that my suffering was not in vain.

I was compelled to search deeper for the answers just to survive the battle raging within. I needed to know whether my life after paralysis had a purpose, and what that purpose might be. I needed to find a reason to want to get up in the morning, to face the challenges of each day, and a reason to want to live in this new existence. So I threw myself into studying the Word of God, and other related books, in search of answers and to clarify the ambiguities.

I was in a unique position in my life, where I could easily withdraw from the busyness of this world and immerse in studying. After all, there was nothing else pressing in my life! Placing a book on my bedside table, I mustered enough strength to turn the page with a hand stick. Little by little, some of the mysteries of the Bible were becoming clearer to me.

One day, I had a visit from Pastor Farhad's wife, Sheri. She introduced me to the story of "Joni."[9] I knew very little about Joni Eareckson Tada, as I had only heard her on the radio a few times on my way to work. It is so ironic that I only learned about her paralysis and life in a wheelchair just a few weeks prior to my accident! Her book was about her struggles with accepting life in a wheelchair after a diving accident at the age of seventeen. Her book inspired me; the story of how God had used her circumstances for a much greater good. She has touched the lives of millions of people around the world with all the different ministries she is managing.

In the hospital my only hope was a miraculous healing. After reading Joni's story, and other books in search of answers, I began to see that the purpose of our lives and everything that happens, fits into a much larger picture that God has designed for eternity.

---

[9] Joni: An Unforgettable Story

8

Visions and Dreams

*The strands are woven together in such
a way as to form a beautiful tapestry.*

During those times of intense studying in search of
answers, I began having visions and dreams. The dreams
were scattered across several years. My first profound dream
occurred in June of 1998. I record my dreams in a computer
file called "Spiritual Dreams."

> In this dream, I saw rows and rows of computers
> communicating with each other. These computers
> were so sophisticated that they had freedom of
> choice. They were created to serve MAN, but
> a virus had corrupted their programs, and now
> they only served themselves and their own will.
> In this process, when they faced opposing wills,
> they destroyed the others. Their existence now
> encircled attempts to enforce their will and to
> destroy each other. MAN entered this realm as
> a computer, and offered other computers this
> choice: to allow MAN to destroy the virus and
> to reprogram their corrupted software. And to
> those who chose to allow MAN to destroy the

virus and be reprogrammed, was given a new
existence, not as a computer but as a human.
Other computers who rejected MAN were
eventually destroyed.

When I awakened from this dream, knowing that I
might forget the details, I immediately dictated it to Soheila,
my friend from church, who was living with us and was my
caregiver for a while. She wrote it all down as I dictated to
her, while I was still in bed. It is recorded here exactly as it
was then written (translated).

One night after three days of fasting, Soheila and I
began to pray at nine o'clock, and we continued our prayer
for two hours. I was in bed, and she was sitting on the floor
beside me. She went to bed before midnight, but I just kept
on praising God. I couldn't stop. Words of praise were just
flowing out of me. In the stillness, I completely lost my sense
of time. It seemed only a few minutes had passed, but the
sun was now shining through the window of my bedroom.
It must have been close to six o'clock in the morning. I had
prayed all night! I was in what some Christians refer to as
"the presence of God." I don't know if praise was the key
to being in the presence of God, but God was whispering
to my heart things I had never taken time to hear before (or
more like downloading information into my mind.) I cannot
fully explain it. Perhaps only those who have experienced it
can understand.

For the first time, I heard the voice of God audibly. It
sounded different from hearing my own voice in my head.
A separate entity had entered my mind and was speaking to
me, sometimes in words, and other times in images, or both.
I was in awe, overwhelmed by the possibility of real contact
with God! In the presence of God there was unspeakable

joy, total security, complete satisfaction, and pure love. I was completely satisfied and felt no need for food, water, or sleep. The joy I felt was overflowing, I could not contain it. I remained in this heightened state of awareness all day. I knew that in my physical body I could not possibly continue in this state. And as suddenly as it came, it also vanished as quickly, and I was returned to my familiar world of senses. I did not talk about this experience to anyone. I was afraid they would think I was crazy. Today, I long to return to the thrill of that life-changing encounter.

> I had a vision where I saw myself as a piece in a puzzle in which each piece was alive and active. The pieces were converging, diverging, and scattering in many directions. Although not all the pieces belonged in the puzzle, their existence was absolutely necessary, so that by colliding they ensured the precise position of each piece in the final picture in which the strands are woven together in such a way as to form a beautiful tapestry.

> In another dream, it was as if someone was speaking to me. I was told in the dream that America was built on Christian principles, and it had come to be known around the globe as the land of the free. Then I saw many people flock to America from all over the world in search of freedom. Although evil was allowed to subtly lurk in, some people in search of freedom would meet Christ and find real freedom.

> I dreamt of driving one day with my friends to "The City." As I got out of the car, I noticed

I wasn't wearing shoes, and I felt embarrassed. How was I going to walk on cold and hard pavement of the city streets without shoes? I went to a store and could not find proper shoes. Then I heard a voice saying, "I want to send you to the people, but you're not equipped," and I awoke from the dream. The next morning, I happened to be listening to a sermon by Charles Stanley, a Christian Pastor, and one sentence he uttered captivated me: "You need to be equipped with the Holy Spirit."

In a dream, I saw myself crying out to God. Painfully aware of my weaknesses, in desperation I cried out, "Lord, am I even saved?" Then just as I left the dream I heard a voice saying, "A high price has been paid for your freedom. A very high price indeed."

In one dream, I saw a place where people were traumatized and controlled by fear. They were completely under the dominance of the evil one. He was merciless, utterly devoid of any compassion, and totally driven by cruelty.

I've had many dreams in which I found myself in a field with the softest and most beautiful grass, crystal clear waters, exquisite flowers and colors beyond the limits of my imagination. I saw beautiful houses in the distance, bridges spanning still waters, and happy groups of people walking about. I noticed there was no need for breathing there. There was total peace and complete serenity. I knew in my dream that this place did not exist on Earth.

Although I do not have as many spiritual dreams as I did then, I believe symbols in those dreams have a much more profound and deeper meaning that any one word can convey.

9

A Community Comes Together

"Let your light shine before others, that
they may see your good deeds and glorify
your Father in heaven."
Matthew 5:16

Passively watching others do the housework, I realized
how much effort was involved in managing a household
and in keeping it clean. All the sweeping, mopping, dusting,
and washing seemed to be overwhelming for a caregiver.
I knew I had to simplify my life. I had to give away all the
unnecessary stuff that required extra care. At first, it was
difficult to part with things I had collected over the years
and to which I had become attached. However, once I gave
them away, I felt a sense of freedom. Why did I feel that
I needed to fill my house with all those things anyway?
Buying and collecting stuff can become an obsession. We
buy them, store them, dust them, take care of them, then
we get tired of the clutter and sell them in garage sales, and
we do it all over again. No wonder we never have time for
important things in life!

While some people disappeared from our lives because
they didn't exactly know how to react, others remained.
Our house was in dire need of organization, and our small

church community, neighbors and friends came to help. They cleaned our house, stocked our freezer with home-cooked meals in containers, planted flowers in the front yard, and helped us get organized. A community motivated by love came together.

I have to admit receiving help is humbling. I understand better now the saying: "Giving is better than receiving." I felt a sense of shame from asking for help. But I had to learn to leave pride aside and to accept graciously the much needed help that I was given. I remember crying in the office of one of Shepherd Center's counselors. While gently placing her hands on my shoulders and looking intently into my eyes, she told me there was nothing wrong with someone else helping to brush my teeth, and that there was nothing wrong with someone else helping me to eat. It took a long time for me to come to peace with that. A friend told me it was an honor for her to help me. She said it made her feel needed and good about herself, because someone else needed her. I hadn't thought about it that way!

🦋 🦋 🦋

My mother-in-law, Mahin flew from Iran to stay with us for several months. She is a gentle, patient, loving and positive-minded woman. I feel so blessed to have her in my life. Mahin has faced many difficulties in her own life. She knows much about long suffering. Her third son died of a childhood disease at the age of two. The pain of losing a child is still in her heart when she speaks of him with tears in her eyes. Her last son, Pedram, was born with a very rare heart condition, and the doctors warned he would not survive for very long. Twenty-five years later, with advances in medical technology, he had corrective heart surgery in

Houston, and now lives in Iran. (That's the reason Shahram was in Houston when we met.)

I have learned so much from her wisdom through the years. She encouraged me to learn to do things on my own. She would go on long walks with me outside to help me overcome the fear of being in a wheelchair. She would make me pick up grapes to help me use my fingers. Through her love and compassion, I gained the confidence and strength to face the challenges ahead.

My father-in-law was able to take some time off from his busy law practice, and he soon joined us. During my in-laws' stay, they quietly watched the love and support of our Christian community, and my mother-in-law made the decision to accept Jesus as her savior, finding real freedom right here in America. And I was reminded of this Bible verse: *"Let your light shine before others, that they may see your good deeds and glorify your Father in heaven."* Matthew 5:16. She was later baptized in the same lake that her son was baptized in a few years earlier.

After several months, they flew back to Iran. As they were saying goodbye on their way to the airport, I noticed how beautiful they looked together. In his mid seventies, he was tall and slim, with shoulder length silver hair and blue eyes. Dressed in a three-piece suit, he looked very handsome. She was dressed in a light peach colored outfit, which made her look even more attractive. They had tears in their eyes as they said goodbye. I felt like an orphan; I didn't want them to leave! I was going to miss them. Before leaving, my father-in-law asked my husband what he was going to do.

"I'm going to stay with my wife and take care of her," he replied.

With tears in his eyes he placed one hand on his son's shoulder and said, "That's the way I've raised you. I'm proud of you, son."

So many people came to help. Kathy, my sister-in-law and our friend Joann took me on a road trip back to Houston, so I could visit my family and also get used to traveling. I was paranoid about traveling and felt claustrophobic in an automobile. I don't know how they handled all my moaning and groaning every time a car came too close. Kathy, being the funniest and most loving person I know, soon figured out how to put me at ease. She handed me a bag of sunflower seeds and a bucket to spit out the hard shells. By the end of the trip I had no sense of taste left on my tongue! I nearly choked on a few, however, the trip turned out to be the most wonderful and memorable ever! We still talk and laugh about it.

One day, our friend, Mr. R., who had recently recovered from a massive heart attack that almost took his life, was visiting. He was an older gentleman in his early seventies. Before my accident, my husband used to visit him in his house quite often while they shared Persian tea and played backgammon. He knew we were Christians and thought of us as naïve young kids.

He always had interesting stories about growing up in Iran. He told us about being a mischievous young boy in Iran, who took Bibles from the missionaries and sold the paper to the local grocers to use for wrapping seeds and nuts for sale to the public. Come to find out, one of the young men who bought the seeds actually read the paper in which it was wrapped. He continued to buy more nuts, so he could read more of the Bible, and as a result came in contact with the missionaries, and later became a Christian!

A few more people came to visit that day, and as I was describing my vision of Jesus carrying me in the hospital, the doorbell rang. It was an acquaintance coming to pay me a visit before moving to Los Angeles. She handed me a gift, explaining that she was compelled to purchase it when she first heard about my accident. She said that she saw it in a store window, and it had my name written all over it!

I was stunned when she unwrapped the gift. It was an amazing statue. It was a white statue of Jesus, in the lap of Mary, after his crucifixion. The lifeless body of Jesus was in the loving arms of His sorrowful mother as she tenderly looked upon her beloved son. It was a replica of Michelangelo's "Pieta." The statue was exactly like the vision I saw in the hospital, with the exception of Jesus carrying me! She didn't know anything about my vision, and I hadn't seen her since the accident. Who could have compelled this dear woman to buy this amazing statue for me, but God Himself. The guests were dumbfounded. That statue was a confirmation to everyone that God was there with me in the hospital, and He had indeed been carrying me!

God used special ways to reveal His love to me. Yet my inner struggles made it easy for me to slip into ungratefulness, and enter into the world of "Why me," and "If only . . ."

10

Acceptance

I am beloved by God

I recall the day I saw my reflection in a large glass window at a shopping center. The person looking back at me: sitting in an electric wheelchair, her arms atrophied from lack of movement hanging at her sides, her head leaning a bit forward as she struggled to sit up straight, encased in a monstrosity of metal, plastic, and wires; was this me? In shock, I stared at my reflection. Although it had been several months after my injury, I was not used to seeing myself in a wheelchair. I had not pictured myself quite that way.

Prior to my accident, I did not personally know anyone in a wheelchair. During college, I remember meeting a student in a wheelchair who was slightly slow to speak. One day, he tried to strike up a conversation with me in class. I smiled politely, but I didn't want to give him the time of day. Did I judge him as being less intelligent? Was I ashamed to be seen with him? Or was it a subconscious fear of becoming disabled myself? Seeing my image in the store's glass window brought me face to face with my own prejudice!

My life had been radically altered by the accident, and my biggest struggle, aside from learning to deal with the physical and emotional consequences was redefining my very identity. Unsure of my role in life, I often asked myself this question, "Who am I now?"

Christianity teaches that we find our identity and our significance in God's unchanging love. We have value because of whom God has made us to be. Brennan Manning, in his book, *Abba's Child: The Cry of the Heart for Intimate Belonging,* says, "Define yourself radically as one beloved by God. This is the true self. Every other identity is illusion." Imprisoned by feelings of unworthiness, it was difficult to trust that I was truly loved, yet here was the key to my identity and self-acceptance. I am beloved by God!

I knew I had to change my attitude about myself and make peace with the realities of life with paralysis. I had to adapt to this new way of living, to being in a wheelchair, and to being patient in doing the things that were effortless before the accident. I knew the process of acceptance was not going to be easy by any means, so my prayer became the Serenity Prayer of Reinhold Niebuhr. *"God, give me grace to accept with serenity the things I cannot change, courage to change the things I can, and wisdom to know the difference."*

Change in life is inevitable and much of our suffering results from resisting change. Acceptance is the beginning of adaptation to change. It has taken me years to learn to redefine myself, not by the image I see in the mirror, but by the *person* I am. We are so much more than the image we see. We are so much more than the stuff we own. Our looks, our clothes, our cars, or our jobs don't make us who we are, even though many of us think they do. If our identity is based on these things, we may feel totally lost when we have to give them up. These externals cannot define a human being.

I had to learn to accept myself with all my physical limitations and to make the most of my gifts and abilities.

Acceptance allowed me to have a greater appreciation for those senses that were still available to me. It led to an attitude change from defeat to victory, and from self-pity to mastery. Being able to pick up a book without help became a triumph, "Yes, I did it!" rather than self-pity, where I would say, "Look how long it takes me just to pick up a book!" Acceptance allowed me to learn to love and embrace the person looking back at me through that store's glass window. It also set the stage for the challenge of loving and accepting others.

11

Prayer

Thy will be done

We were struggling with our finances as our debts were mounting. Our rental house in Houston was vacant (After moving to Georgia, we rented our home in Houston.) Due to the enormous amount of care that I required after my accident, we had neglected to periodically check on the condition of that rental house. As a result, our tenant destroyed our property, and we could no longer rent it in that condition. It was being repaired with the help of my brother and his wife, but we had no funds to pay the mortgage.

I have fond memories of that two-story house. The high ceiling and lots of windows made it appear light and airy. Shahram had planted a banana tree in the glass-enclosed atrium, which also helped give the house a tropical appearance. By the way, one year that tree actually produced bananas!

I had been praying for our finances with my friend, Shirin. I met her soon after my accident. She came to visit with Pastor Sasan one day. She had dark hair and beautiful facial features that reminded me of antique paintings of Persian women. During the visit, my mother-in-law, who was visiting us from Iran, discovered that Shirin's parents were their neighbors when they lived in the city of Nahavand in Iran. She knew Shirin's parents quite well. Somehow, we are all connected in this puzzle of life! Later on, Shirin moved in with us and helped to care for me while she attended seminary school. During her stay, we often talked about her adventurous life.

Shirin had attended both high school and college in France, before moving to Norway, where she finished her graduate studies in chemistry. She became a Christian while temporarily staying in a monastery in France, after the Iranian Revolution, when money coming from Iran was scarce. And now, she was studying theology in America. She spoke four languages quite well.

One night at about 11 p.m., Shirin and I began praying for many things, including our rental house in Houston. I desperately wanted to be freed from that obligation, so it wasn't the first time I had prayed for our house.

The next morning, I was working on my computer while sipping my coffee. Using a mouse with trackball and hand devices that allowed me to type, I was surfing the Internet when the phone rang. It was our old tenant! Needless to say I was not pleased to hear from her.

"Has anyone told you what has happened? I guess the neighbors did not know who to call, so they contacted me," she said.

Uninterested in conversing with her, I asked, "What are you talking about?"

"You don't know? Last night there was a storm and your house was hit by lightning. It was the only house that caught on fire and burned to the ground," she said.

I was stunned! I couldn't believe what I was hearing. I called the neighbor in Houston to talk to her. She said her son was up and saw everything. A bolt of lightning hit our house at about 10 p.m. that night. Ten o'clock in Houston is 11 p.m. in Atlanta. That is the exact time that Shirin and I were praying!

I called my family in Houston and asked them to drive by the house to take a look for us. My sister called me back.

"Nasrin, you won't believe it. Your house is burned to the ground but the pine tree (which was only a few feet from the house) was not touched. Even the bushes in the front yard are not burned," she said.

The much-needed money we received from the insurance and from selling the land covered our expenses for months to come! Shirin and I have remained good friends and prayer partners. From time to time, we recall that night of fervent prayers.

I often wondered why God answers some prayers in miraculous ways and other times He seems quiet. Why didn't God answer the prayers of so many people for my healing? Through the years I have learned to trust God because I know that He loves me, even when His answer to my prayer is "No." We live in a complex world and I don't know the best possible outcome for every event, or its consequences; only God knows. Therefore, instead of "my will be done" in prayer, I can say "Thy will be done."

12

Bible Translation

*If you want to help your people, come,
and follow me.*

The first Bible I ever had was in Farsi. A student in high school had given it to me after I moved to America over 35 years ago. I began reading it but had a difficult time understanding it, because it was an old translation. So, I lost interest in continuing to read it. Years later, when I became a Christian, I discovered that the Persian Bible I was given was a revised version of the first translation that was printed in 1895, by the British and Foreign Bible Society.

The New Testament, as well as parts of the Old Testament, had since been translated into modern Persian language. The United Bible Societies were searching for an Iranian to translate the remaining parts of the Old Testament into modern Persian language. Dr. Kenneth Thomas was the United Bible Societies' Translation Consultant for the Today's Persian Version Bible translation project.

Pastor Sasan had approached Shahram about applying for the job of translating parts of the Old Testament into Farsi. Shahram had translated books before and was knowledgeable in literature and Persian language. He was to submit a selected sample translation for their approval.

He never got around to doing it until those long days in the hospital, when he finally translated the selected passages. He sent the sample translation to all the members of the committee for their review and recommendation. A few weeks later he received a phone call from the committee. His translation was chosen!

God had miraculously provided him with a job of translating the Bible! This meant that he would not only be able to stay home and take care of me, but also be able to financially provide for us. The irony is that God had chosen the person who had ripped the Bible into pieces a few years earlier, to now translate the same book! Perhaps this was the way he was going to help his people, as he saw in the dream of Jesus telling him, "If you want to help your people, come, and follow me."

After many years of hard work with a large team of translators, typesetters, editors, exegetical checkers, proofreaders, support and technical staff, the translation was completed in 2007. *Today's Persian Version* of the Bible was printed and is now in the hands of the people in Iran. My husband attended the inauguration to introduce it worldwide and dedicate this translation to Persian speaking ministries, which was held in August of 2007 in Turkey.

Pastor Sasan before moving to England to work on his Ph.D., introduced us to many Christian books to translate into Farsi. My brother-in-law, Pedram, who had the heart operation years before and now lived in Iran was a good candidate for translating one of the books, so we sent it to him to translate. After losing the translation to a computer virus and having to retranslate it all over again, he called one night with special news. He said that through the translation he had realized that he, too, had been the prodigal son. Through the translation he accepted Christ as his savior!

13

A Hidden Talent

*A gift from God to be discovered at
such a time as this.*

My life had drastically changed from being active and
engaged, to being idle, lounging around the house. So I
desperately needed to find something to do. I associated
meaning in life with activities, which meant constantly doing
something. So, being confined to a wheelchair and not even
being able to use my hands, was devastating. I needed to
do something that would challenge my mind and use my
creativity; I needed to somehow express myself.

My husband suggested painting. At first, I was reluctant.
My response to him was, "I can't even feed myself, how can
I paint?" Also, I had no known artistic talent. In college I
had dabbled at a painting or two for my room, but nothing
serious. Inspired by my sister, Fari, who was a talented
artist, I took art history in college and became familiar with
various styles of art. My favorite art style was surrealism,
and "The Persistence of Memory" by Salvador Dali was
my favorite painting. Not being able to use my fingers, and
having limited use of my dominant right arm, painting
seemed impossible.

However, on a beautiful fall day in Georgia, when the leaves transformed to vibrant colors of red and yellow, I felt inspired to paint, so I decided to give it a try. Using a hand brace in my left arm, with the help of my shoulder and arm muscles, I was able to hold a paint brush (I had to learn to do everything using my left arm.) With sweeping strokes, I began painstakingly painting. Soon I was spending hours painting, day after day. I had found an avenue to express my creativity and it felt really good. While painting, my mind was free of thought, my emotions were open, and I was able to focus. To my amazement, my painting improved in a short time!

Inspired by paintings by contemporary landscape artists, Howard Behrens, Sung Kim, and Robert Wood, I began painting scenery using acrylics. Over time, as I gained more strength in my arm, I moved on to oil painting on canvas.

I immersed myself in art. Sometimes, the only thing that stopped me from painting was the dull pain I felt in my neck and shoulders after painting for several hours. I had discovered a hidden talent and a passion for painting. I found myself being carried into the scenery, and I began living in my art creations! I saw myself sipping coffee at a sidewalk café in a seaport village along the blue breezy Mediterranean Sea. I saw myself running through lush green grass in an open field, overlooking log cabins at a distance. I saw myself walking on the sidewalk alongside a river in a charming town, with the moon casting its light on the still waters. I was there, and could feel and sense the landscape.

Our hidden talents need an opportunity to be discovered. Having a busy corporate life, I had never taken the time nor had any inclination to discover this gift. Perhaps it was a gift from God to be discovered at such a time as this!

Finding something I was good at and enjoyed gave me the passion and confidence I needed at the time. Painting has become a part of my ministry and my life message demonstrating God's power working through me.

If you are in a time of adversity, begin to explore your hidden gifts and talents. You might be surprised! There are countless possibilities. I try to encourage others to paint. My mother says she doesn't have the talent for painting. However, she likes baking. She likes making her own art that tastes good too, and that's wonderful.

14

A Time to Learn

*By reaching out to others, you would
find healing for yourself.*

When the weather was nice, I spent a lot of time outdoors. With plenty of sunshine and fresh air, I felt free and independent. So when our upper deck was made accessible, it became my sanctuary. My husband hung several wind chimes in various locations and covered the deck with numerous pots of flowers of exquisite colors. The lovely melodic sounds of the wind chimes, mixed with the calm gurgling of rushing water from the creek below, and the scent of the flowers breezing in the air welcomed me every morning, as I wheeled onto the deck to read a book or to just enjoy the solitude.

As I felt more confident, I went for "strolls" in my wheelchair in our quiet neighborhood by myself. One day a neighbor asked me to visit her mother who had suffered a stroke and was now confined to a wheelchair. She was in her seventies and afraid to leave her house, so during our visits I tried to encourage her to become more independent. I never imagined I would be a source of hope and encouragement for someone else; however, I noticed her attitude slowly changing. I was elated the day I saw her in her wheelchair, merrily riding around the neighborhood, all by herself!

I had just discovered a secret. By reaching out to others, I would find healing for myself. Also, when we help others without expectation, we receive help when we need it. That help may not always be from those whom we helped in the past. Most of the time, it comes from different people in different forms. Through this same neighbor I met Lauren, a massage therapist who has remained my loyal friend for almost seven years. She is the most loving and cheerful person I know. Besides relieving my pain and healing my body with her anointed fingers, she has taught me a lot about receiving guidance and direction from God. Another longtime friend, Moe, has built a ramp in the back of his house to make it easy for me to visit his home. He often invites us to enjoy his famous barbeque, and fresh fruits and vegetables from his garden. A life of sharing and giving of ourselves by small acts of kindness and thoughtfulness, leads to joy.

Through the years, I have had many caregivers. Today I have a wonderful caregiver. Ruth is from the Kikuyu tribe of Kenya. I have known her for more than seven years. Loyalty, responsibility and discipline are rare virtues, which she possesses. I have learned so much about the wonderful people of Kenya and their noble tribal customs and traditions.

However, living with different caregivers can be challenging. The relationship can sometimes be worse than marriage! You quickly discover that you can really get on each other's nerves. Often I wondered why I had so many difficult people around me. "God, get me away from these people!" I screamed. But I soon discovered that they were there for a purpose. God has used many difficult people in my life, to help me see myself and to change. We are like mirrors reflecting each other's image. If I saw something in others that aggravated me, most likely it was the reflection of my own weakness or flaw. And that's the way we sharpen one another. As soon as I changed, I noticed my circumstances changed; that difficult person disappeared, or they no longer seemed so difficult after all!

Being totally dependent, it also became essential for me to learn to express my needs. I was appalled at how often I was misunderstood. "God, why can't they understand what I'm saying?" I had to learn to openly express my thoughts, rather than to suppress them, which often led to frustrations that would be later expressed in the wrong way, at the wrong time. I noticed that sometimes, my motivation was just to win the argument. I had to learn to resist the desire to prove that I was always right.

Years of being dependent on others for my every need, has taught me not to expect others to do everything my way. My husband made me aware that I was becoming extremely demanding and controlling. That's what expectations do, and when left unfulfilled they can lead to disappointment, frustration, and anger. My expectations of others were unrealistic in relationship to what they were capable of providing. If you want less frustration in your life, change your expectations and begin to accept what you receive from others as a privilege and not a right. I now appreciate what my husband does for me, rather than expecting him to do it just because he is my husband. Although sometimes I still slip-up, I am more at peace and experience less frustration when I show a grateful attitude instead. And you know what? I discovered that once I adopted this new attitude, people love to please me and do things for me!

In the message book from my days in the hospital, there is a beautiful note from my sister Simin, which years later made perfect sense to me.

> *". . . God will bring you different people for different purposes. If someone is only capable of giving you love, allow them to only give you love and nothing else. Don't expect people to do things they are incapable of doing; they end up doing harm rather than good."*

Such words of wisdom!

15

Compassion

*A compassionate attitude comes from a
broken heart.*

Being physically challenged has many obstacles. One
is dressing, so I designed fashionable, wrap-around skirts
for myself that used Velcro fasteners and asked my friend,
Fereshteh, who was an accomplished seamstress, to sew the
skirts for me.

Fereshteh came to America from Iran and soon after was
introduced to me by a friend. At that time, I was looking for
a caregiver, and she ended up living with us and helped with
my care for over a year. She was a devout Muslim with her
hair covered at all times. Throughout the months she lived
in our home, we spoke often about Christian beliefs; she
also helped my husband with the typing of the translations
of the Bible. Her observation was that Jesus' teaching in the
Bible was easy to understand, but very difficult to practice.
My response to her was that it's impossible to practice
without the spirit of Christ empowering us.

Years later, she told me that just before leaving Iran
for the United States, one day she happened to walk past
a church. For reasons unknown to her, she felt compelled
to walk into the church, kneel down by the pew and pray.

Her prayer went something like this, "Dear Jesus, I am coming to your country and I don't know very many people there. Please take care of me yourself." Ever since then, Jesus has been working in her life. She later became a Christian and was baptized. She has been an angel in my life and a most loyal friend. Incidentally, her name means Angel in Farsi!

I asked Fereshteh to sew several skirts and took them to Shepherd hospital one day. I wanted to share the idea of the Velcro skirts with other newly paralyzed women. On the way to the hospital, I felt a strong urge to visit my old hospital room. I didn't know why I wanted to return there, but when I entered the room, I knew why! Sometimes, we are not sure if it is God or us who is leading, but in retrospect we can tell.

Lying on the bed in that room was a young woman about my own age, hooked up to all kinds of tubes and machines, unable to do anything for herself. The familiar fear of an unknown future emanated from her eyes. Her elderly parents were in the room with her. I introduced myself, and asked her how she came to be there. Ironically, she was involved in a car accident on her way back from skiing in Colorado. She was then transferred to Shepherd Center in Atlanta.

I told her I had spent most of my time at Shepherd in that very room. I gave her one of the skirts, my phone number, told her about painting, and cheerfully encouraged her about all the things she could still do. Before leaving, I prayed for her to be off the respirator and able to breathe on her own. I knew exactly how she felt and recognized her need to know that there is life after paralysis.

I visited her a second time, but the third time I went to the hospital she had been released. The nurse told me that before leaving the hospital, she was able to breathe on her own without a respirator. Answered prayer! Thank you, Lord.

My trips to the hospital continued. I visited many patients and shared my paintings with them. Knowing that they probably felt disoriented about time and dates, I made a calendar of my paintings on my computer, and gave them the printout so they could hang it on the wall of their hospital room. I encouraged them and prayed for them. Some patients were receptive and others were not, yet that did not discourage me.

A few months later I received a phone call. It was the lady from Colorado I met in my old hospital room. I asked her how she was doing. She told me that soon after her recovery she had gone back to her old job as the director of a nursing home. She is now an active member of a church, and is involved in fundraising for the Christopher Reeve Foundation. She said when I entered into her hospital room that day, she knew that God had sent me to encourage her. I hung up the phone with tears in my eyes, and I thanked God for enabling me to make a difference in someone else's life.

A compassionate attitude comes from a broken heart. Our suffering enables us to reach out to others, understand their pain, and offer comfort.

16

Lasting Friendships

*There are times when we need to
console others, as well as times when we
ourselves need to be consoled.*

There are times when God steps in and solves a problem
that seems impossible. At a car auction when my husband
was shopping for an accessible van, he met a gentleman who
needed a ride home. During the ride, they talked about my
accident. He introduced us to Lance Cooper, an attorney
who discovered that the severity of my injury was due to
a faulty seatbelt in the car I was driving. He helped us to
reach a settlement. The annuity has provided for most of
my monthly expenses.

Now that we were financially independent and I had
a fulltime Certified Nurse's Assistant, my husband had
more free time to pursue his art work. His art gave him
the much-needed relief from the stresses associated
with care giving. It was then that he met Sofia, a Russian
artist. Together they developed many art works right in
the basement of our house, including an 18 feet by 6 feet
bas-relief sculpture of the Last Supper, with a modern
twist featuring disciples as Abraham Lincoln, Martin Luther
King, Jr., Billy Graham, Harriet Tubman, and Mother

Teresa. Ordered by Fred and Yvonne Milani (Yvonne had washed my hair when I was in the hospital), this relief was placed in the banquet hall of their newly constructed home, the White House of Georgia.

Our house was becoming a safe haven, a place for people to come and share meals, create art, discuss personal concerns, Christian perspectives, and other aspects of life. There was a spirit of freedom and informality, which made everyone feel at ease. We welcomed all who came. We had discovered the strength to persevere, despite our circumstances, and that provided hope for many. Perhaps that's why they came! Pastor Farhad's wife, Sheri would comment that our house had become like the L'Abri.[10]

People brought their friends, and I met so many wonderful people. Our capacity to love and share was divinely expanded, and I found myself connecting with others in ways that I would never have thought possible. Our lives were greatly enriched with culture, friendships, and love. We now had friends from Brazil, Kenya, Czech Republic, Romania, Russia, and other countries. One night we had a guest from the Zulu tribe of South Africa, who performed the traditional tribal dance right in our living room, as I played the tambourine, and others played along with drums. Afterwards, we enjoyed a delicious meal of chicken with mango and kiwi sauce, prepared by one of the visitors who was a chef at a famous restaurant in Atlanta.

---

[10] L'Abri is a French word that means shelter, a place where people might find satisfying answers to their questions and practical demonstration of Christian care. It was founded in Switzerland in 1955 by Dr. Francis Schaeffer, a Christian theologian and philosopher.

Some days we had a dozen visitors, and they had to park their cars and walk a long way to the house. Some people stayed with us for days or weeks when they needed healing during a time of emotional difficulty in their lives. Many life changing conversations took place there. There are times when we need to console others, as well as times when we ourselves need to be consoled. By learning to listen, understanding their pain, and investing in their success, we build supportive relationships.

One summer, a friend's son came to stay with us for a while. He was 23 years old and had just gone through Alcoholic Anonymous. When he first came he was weary, seemed depressed, and uncertain about his future. We spent time walking by his side, helping him navigate his future. Together we talked, cooked meals, read books and poems, laughed, and even cried. In between backgammon games with my husband, they discussed the more serious aspects of life. In a non-judgmental and encouraging environment, God helped him get back on the right track. Today he is free of all addictions, his mind is sound, and he is pursuing his Ph.D. in psychology, while working with troubled teenagers suffering from drug addiction. God takes us out of our darkness so that we can become a light for others!

I believe the life that God has intended for us is a life of interdependence and not independence. Our life of interdependence actually led to the establishment of deeper relations with others. Once-superficial connections with acquaintances became thoughtful relationships, as we became more transparent, no longer fearing to admit our imperfections. Those relationships transformed into enduring friendships. Looking back, that was a special season in our lives, one that lasted several years, years I will always cherish.

17

A Special Union

God has given us a daughter!

It was the summer of 2004. The weather in Georgia was hot and sticky. After spending the day outdoors, I decided to go to bed early to rest and watch a movie. After a while, my husband walked into the bedroom with a blank look on his face. He sat on the bed beside me and abruptly said, "I got a phone call from my daughter."

I was engrossed watching the movie, so I didn't pay much attention and just said, "What?"

"I got a phone call from my daughter."

I didn't know what he was talking about. In confusion I asked, "What are you talking about?"

"I have a daughter."

"We have a daughter?"

"Yes." He began explaining.

"I knew her mother in college. After I came back from Iran, before I met you, we saw each other again and were in a relationship. She became pregnant, but I knew I did not want children, and I was not emotionally ready for such a responsibility. She moved to her parents' home in Oklahoma and raised the baby by herself. We were never in contact with each other. She is now 15 years old and wants to come and visit us."

Without hesitation, I said, "That's great! God has given us a daughter." And I really meant it. How ironic! He ran away from responsibility and ended up with a wife who is totally dependent on him . . . and now a daughter.

Weeks later, we both went to the airport to pick her up. Her name is Celia. She had a petite figure, blue eyes, and soft, dark-brown hair with streaks of blond. She was so lovely with the sweetest spirit. I fell in love with her the moment I saw her. I didn't sense any resentment or bitterness on her part, which was something I was concerned about.

She had searched the Internet and had decided to contact him at this time in her life. The timing was perfect, because God had prepared my heart through this journey and had stretched my capacity to love. I'm not sure if I would have been able to accept this so easily earlier. My insecurities and jealous tendencies would have prevented me from opening my heart to her.

We bonded immediately. She visited us during the summer months, and we grew closer each time she came to visit. In some ways, she was so much like her dad. Today, Celia is a young lady in college, and I love her dearly.

Incidentally, she is attending the same University from which I graduated. We are both OU football team fans. She called me on Mother's Day this year and wished me a happy day. I must be doing something right! I am in touch with Bonnie, Celia's mother, by phone and email. I think she has done a wonderful job of raising Celia.

We have to face the consequences of our past behavior. We must take responsibility for our actions and allow God's forgiveness to wash away our guilt. Jesus has provided adequate provision for our sin and our guilt. We can either play the game of blame, shame and guilt, or we can fall into the arms of our Heavenly Father and take the responsibility for making things right.

No relationship can remain unaffected by events of life, and our marriage was no exception. Discovering and adjusting to our new roles was one of the most difficult aspects of our marriage. Unable to do some of the things I used to do for my husband was especially painful. Our circumstance has forced us to redefine our marriage. Although at the beginning of my injury we grew much closer, like most relationships, problems arose through the years from poor communication. Sometimes we suppress our thoughts and emotions for fear of being rejected. When honest and open communications break down, we tend to hide our inner worlds from each other, and misunderstandings can occur. Instead of being angry and disrespectful, we had to learn to resolve our conflicts in ways that would restore and sustain our love and respect for each other.

Shahram has his own struggles in life and issues that he must resolve. Sometimes, when he shuts me out of his world and I feel unloved and unwanted, I crawl into the heart of God and remain there until I can hear Him call me *His beloved*. I am God's beloved!

Despite the difficulties, we have ministered together to hurting people, brought hope to their lives, and helped them go through their storms of life a little easier. We've been on this journey together. Too many people find it easier to give up. They give up on their spouses, on their kids, on their friends and on themselves. Yet, if we find the courage to face our problems, persevere, and take small steps to resolve them, we find that there is nothing impossible with God. I pray that we keep God in the center of our lives, so that our relationship will not end in separation or divorce, like so many of today's couples.

18

Paradigm Shift

"Do not conform to the pattern of this world,
but be transformed by the renewing
of your mind."

Romans 12:2

After painting for several months, I had more paintings than I knew what to do with. At that time, quite accidentally, I became involved with our church's publication. At first, I provided my paintings for use in the publication, then one day I had an urge to write. With the help of hand braces that allowed me to type with two fingers, I began to write. The words flowed as I began typing. It was painfully slow at first, but soon I had a collection of articles in Farsi. A friend helped me to develop a website for my paintings, my testimony, and some articles about the hope we have in Christ.

Soon, I was receiving emails from some people in Iran inquiring about this hope. Many wanted to know how to become a Christian, some were searching, and others wanted advice and counseling. One email was from a woman who had suffered many rejections in her life, by her parents and later her husband, who had left her for another woman. She had been contemplating suicide, and was introduced to my site by her friend. She could not find a reason to live, and she wanted my advice. There were also others who asked for financial help!

Eventually, the correspondence became overwhelming, so I asked others in our church to help me respond. At the same time, many people facing various difficulties and challenges in life were coming to us for advice. I felt inadequate at counseling these people.

My husband suggested that I go back to college to study counseling. Pastor Sasan, who has been so instrumental in our lives, suggested a Christian university in Atlanta that offered Master's degrees in professional counseling and therapy. Psychology had always remained my passion, but I couldn't see how it would be possible for me to go back to college. There were so many obstacles. For one thing, since my caregiver could not come early in the morning to get me ready, I could not start classes earlier than 10 a.m. I would only be able to take classes between times when I had to be "cathetered." This meant I would be limited to attend one class daily. It would take me several years to graduate! Would I be able to ever finish? After all, graduate study can be intensive, and very expensive.

Despite my apprehension, I requested my transcripts from the other universities I had attended, got my references and recommendations, wrote my autobiography, and on the last day of admissions at 4 p.m., I wheeled into the office of the Richmont Graduate University (Psychological Studies Institute at the time) and handed in my papers. Weeks later, I received a letter of acceptance, and I was off to school with my laptop! It was in the fall semester 2003 that I began my classes. During orientation I noticed many of the students were older. Hearing their stories of how a tragic event had compelled them to change their paths gave me a warm sense of belonging.

From the beginning, I dove into my studies with vigor, and gained confidence with every new course. In one of my courses, the professor walked in the first day, opened her Bible and read the following verses: "*Do not conform to the pattern of this world, but be transformed by the renewing of your mind.*" Romans 12:2. She then closed her Bible and looked straight at us and said, "We are going to teach you how to do that!"

The course was about a therapeutic procedure to help discover and change dysfunctional thought patterns that can lead to depression, anxiety, paranoia, and many other disorders. Cognitive therapy, developed by Aaron T. Beck, is a psychological model for improving our mood and behavior. As in my dream of the computers, our software needs reprogramming of the "If . . . and then" statements ingrained in our thought processes.

Our distorted thinking and belief system influences our emotions, and consequently our behavior. By recognizing our distorted view of reality and replacing it with a more realistic and positive view, we can change our behavior. Meditating on negative thoughts leads to the development of negative patterns of thinking. It is a kind of thinking that dreads the future, because it predicts it negatively and ignores all evidence to the contrary. It is a kind of thinking that minimizes the positive accomplishments and exaggerates the negative, the kind of thinking that labels self or others unreasonably and over-generalizes, and on and on . . .

We are living in a mental world created by our thoughts. The destructive thoughts that lead to negative feelings such as helplessness or worthlessness hold us captive and limit our vision of life's possibilities. We are held captives in the prison of our minds! Jesus came to set the captives free. The Bible tells us to guard our mind and to meditate on pure thoughts, so that we can experience the peace of God.

I was battling with periodic bouts of depression and discovered many dysfunctional thought patterns that often contributed to these feelings. We are not immune from negative and destructive thoughts, but when we learn to identify them and recognize their patterns, we can begin to change. Now, when I suddenly feel sad, I examine the thoughts that immediately preceded the sadness. Our negative emotions must not be ignored or suppressed; they should be examined and evaluated, so we can discover the root cause and begin to change. Through observing our emotions, we can detect our wrong thinking and unhealthy attitudes, so that instead of being overwhelmed, we can begin to focus on solutions.

Although psychology does not give the entire answer to the human condition, it does provide care for our mental and emotional needs. While I did not graduate, what I learned has been invaluable for my emotional healing, as well as for helping others.

I soon experienced how our thoughts affect our emotions. In the midst of adversity, we may experience anger and resentment; so it was with me! I recall one day being especially frustrated, because my wheelchair was not working properly and needed repair. As a result, I had to spend a couple of days in bed while it was being fixed.

Being confined to a wheelchair with all its limitations, and now to a bed, was bitter imprisonment. "God, my life is hard enough as it is; why do I have to go through this?" A whirlwind of negative thoughts began racing through my mind. Emotions running wild, I became angry, angry with life and angry with God. Feelings of abandonment and isolation overwhelmed me. I was allowing negative thoughts to completely drive my emotions.

It is what we THINK, not what happens to us, that is always the source of our emotions. It is the way we perceive our circumstances that determines our mood, and consequently, our behavior. Instead of seeing this as an opportunity to meditate, to read, or just to rest, I saw it as life treating me cruelly. The battle is in our minds! Did I like the world I had created for myself? A life of frustration and anger? I knew I needed to reexamine my thought life. What I needed was a paradigm shift in thinking about my paralysis.

It is not possible to get rid of all the frustrations, but I had to decide what was really worth getting upset about, and what wasn't. I had to view some things as simply inconvenient, and not be frustrated. I had to learn to change my attitude about my paralysis and all the nuisances associated with it. I had a choice to make. I could remain bitter, angry, and miserable, or learn to be patient, thankful, and peaceful instead.

For a long time, I couldn't understand why I had to be thankful. Why should I be thankful when life had treated me wrongly? Why should I praise God under these circumstances? But after facing many situations that resulted in my feelings of anger and frustration, I realized the purpose for being thankful. It is to change one way of thinking for another, which actually transforms us. It leads to a new attitude of humbleness and gratefulness, which brings about peace.

Instead of wallowing in ungratefulness and harboring the negative attitude of "why me," I came out of my cocoon and broadened my outlook on life. I began focusing on all the positive aspects of my life. When my attitude shifted, I discovered a freedom and peace that brought a new level of joy.

So, on the day I was confined to bed, I decided to read instead of moaning. I read an article about two boys, ages 10 and 12, who had lost both of their parents to AIDS in a remote village in Africa. They ended up living by themselves and taking care of each other. How can I complain about anything when I read about two little boys, alone much of the time, without enough food, without adequate clothing, and yet able to praise God for the privilege of having shoes so they can walk a mile to school? With tears running down my cheeks, I prayed.

"Oh God, forgive me for my ungratefulness and complaints. You have cared for me, comforted me, provided for me and sustained me. Thank you for your mercy and grace. Lord, bless those two little boys in Africa. Amen."

19

A House on a Hill

God had other plans

Since my accident, more than ten years ago, we had been looking for a one-story ranch house. The house that we owned was a two-story house with a basement. All the bedrooms were on the second floor. After the accident, since I couldn't go upstairs, we had converted our living room into a bedroom. We also remodeled a shower outside of my room near the kitchen to be accessible for my shower chair. Every day for nine years, I was wheeled down the hallway and through the kitchen to take a shower. So it was time to look for a new accessible home.

One day, as I was surfing the Internet in search of a house for sale, I saw an ad for a house on the side of a mountain overlooking the city of Atlanta. I remember when we first moved to Atlanta and were looking to buy a house, we would drive through different neighborhoods, wishing that we could buy this house or that house. Driving on the main street, we could see a neighborhood where the houses were built on the side of a small mountain. I secretly wished that one day I could live in one of those houses overlooking the city. So, when I saw the ad for this house, I told my husband we should check it out. He said it was overpriced, and we could not afford it. But I convinced him to just look. So we called the real estate agent.

When we drove to the neighborhood, we discovered it was the same house I had secretly wished to live in years earlier! The view was breathtaking. Expansive windows provided a panoramic view of downtown Atlanta and the surrounding cities, and created the feeling of being outdoors. Wheeling onto the deck, I felt as though I could almost touch the clouds. But we knew we couldn't afford it, so we didn't think any more about it.

But God had other plans! A few months later, we saw the same house back on the market and the price was reduced. Before we could make an offer, the house went under contract with another buyer, so we gave up again. Then, after a few more months, we saw the house back on the market again, with the price reduced even further! Apparently, the previous deals fell through. This time we took action. We made an offer that we could live with, and they accepted. And all along, we had been praying for God to show us the house we should buy.

In October of 2006, we moved into our dream home. It was still a two-story house with a finished basement; however, this house was large enough to install an elevator.

I love my house. It is an inspiring place for me to create my art work and to write. While we have a lot of parties with friends, when alone I gaze admiringly outside at the art of God, the remarkable cloud formations across the sky, the occasional double rainbow when the sun shines on the droplets of moisture in the air after a rain storm, and the dramatic sight of a golden full moon with the stars in the night sky. At times like this, I feel like the most fortunate person on earth.

20

Doubt

*Nothing in this world, but God Himself,
can satisfy a spirit that has been
awakened.*

It wasn't long after we settled into our new home, that one morning, while sitting at my computer checking my messages, the phone rang. I answered, "Hello?"

A small voice with an unfamiliar accent said, "Hello, is this Nasrin?"

"Yes."

"Maybe I have a wrong number; I don't know, but were you at Shepherd hospital?"

"Yes."

"I was next door to you in the hospital, do you remember me . . . ?"

Immediately, I recognized her. It was Kim, the Korean woman from Shepherd hospital who was suffering from a spinal cord injury and paralysis from the waist down. I remembered the last time I had seen her. It was after we were both released from the hospital and we were in rehabilitation. She was going through an intensive exercise program using parallel bars to try to learn to walk and regain mobility. One day she opened up and talked to me.

"You don't understand. I have children; I am the one who takes them to the mall, to the movies, to different events. What am I gonna' do now? I can't do anything!" she said.

"Oh, but there are so many more important things you can do. You can teach your children to become compassionate, loving, decent human beings, which only you can teach them to be," I replied. I saw a glimpse of hope in her tearful eyes as we parted.

I had not seen her since those days in rehab over 10 years ago. "How are you?" I asked.

"Surviving," she said.

I asked her what she had been doing lately. She explained that their children were all in college, living away from home. Most of her time was spent alone at home, while her husband worked. She said that she was content and had found peace. Her husband, however, was dealing with a lot of anger. I sensed the desperation in her voice. She remembered my husband talking to him in the hospital, and she was wondering if he could talk to him again. I asked for her telephone number, and Shahram called to talk to him.

We invited them for dinner one night. They brought two dozen red roses, and a huge box of assorted candies, cheeses, olives and cookies. We were delighted to see each other. It didn't seem at all that 10 years had gone by. I had forgotten how beautiful she was, with her silky black hair and soft facial features of a porcelain doll. She walked slowly, somewhat dragging herself with the aid of two canes. After sitting around the dining room table, we discussed their lives after her injury. He mentioned that they had gone through even more hardship. He now had doubts whether Jesus was "The Way."

"You have a strong faith," he said.

"It is not that my faith is so strong, but it is the substance of my faith that has kept me standing in the storms of life," I replied. "Let me give you an example about faith that I heard years ago. Let's say there is a lake that is covered with ice, and you need to cross it. No matter how much faith you have, it will not keep you from drowning if the ice is not thick enough to handle your weight. You see, faith is necessary in order for you to step onto the frozen lake, but it is the ice beneath your feet, what you put your faith into, that will either keep you standing in the storms of life, or cause you to drown."

"Our journey is a difficult one," I went on to say. "This is how I see it. Suppose we are in a swamp, our feet in quicksand, going down slowly. Some of us realize our condition because we are so deep in the wet and sticky mud that it's making it hard for us to breathe. Some of us, who are not yet deep enough, are so distracted by the beauty of the leaves and trees surrounding it, that we don't even realize we are in a swamp! Our lusts, desires, and pleasures of life keep us from realizing the depth of the swamp. Nor do we realize our need for deliverance. God extends His arm from heaven down into the swamp, and whispers *"Take hold of my hand and I will save you."* For those of us who take His hand, we'll be lifted out of the swamp. However, now that we are out of the swamp, our bodies are covered with sticky mud, and He has to wash off the dirt; our hearts and minds have to be cleansed and purified. And this process will take the rest of our lives. You see, Jesus is the hand of God extended from heaven into the swamp."

"I never heard it explained this way before," he said.

"Reach out and take His hand; He promises to never let you go."

"What happens to all those left in the swamp?" he asked.

"I don't know! But I'm not gonna take the chance to figure it out."

In many ways, I saw myself in him; remembering times when I doubted or was angry with God. God is not threatened by our anger or doubts. My doubts after the accident forced me to take a closer look at my faith, to clear away misconceptions. My personal experience over the years has shown me that when I move away from God, I get caught in a seemingly inescapable cycle of doubt, worry and anxiety. But when I allow God to embrace me, I feel empowered, peaceful and hopeful.

Nothing in this world, but God Himself, can satisfy a spirit that has been awakened. The most precious thing in the world to me is having a relationship with God through Jesus Christ. I truly believe that fullness of life, peace and joy, in this world of chaos is only possible through this relationship. Jesus brings the gift of wholeness to anyone willing to accept it.

I suggested some books to help him better understand the foundational beliefs of Christianity: the belief that there is a personal, loving God who is ultimately revealed in and through Jesus Christ, who has provided the gift of eternal life and salvation to the world. I believe that the Christian viewpoint offers the best and most hopeful explanation of why things are the way they are. There is plenty of evidence to support it, if we only look closer. Our faith need not be blind, but be reasonable.

Kim and I talk on the phone every now and then, and she always asks me the same question, "Have you finished your book yet? I want to come to your book signing engagement."

21

Forgiveness

*When we forgive, we actually free ourselves
from the pain the abuse caused.*

At times, I had to use a healthcare agency in town to find qualified caregivers. One of my live-in caregivers was an older woman whom I hired through an agency. She seemed sweet and kind, so I hired her right away. She had recently moved from Alabama and needed a place to live. A few weeks after hiring her, we decided to spend the winter in Florida to get away from the cold weather. Having a spinal cord injury, my body is sensitive to cold or hot and cannot regulate its own temperature. The sunshine state, with its beautiful white sandy beaches and turquoise ocean, seemed to offer the best choice.

We stayed in a rental beach house in Florida for a couple of months. My caregiver accompanied us on our trip. During our stay, we relaxed and enjoyed breath-taking sunsets by the beach, visited many art galleries and other attractions, and I had a chance to paint the beauty of some of the beachside scenery. Many friends came to visit and stayed with us for a few days, which made our trip more memorable and fun.

After coming home, while paying the bills I discovered several charges on my credit card at a liquor store in Florida. I also noticed some of my jewelry, including my wedding ring, were missing. I confronted my caregiver, and she confessed. She had pawned my jewelry to pay for her addiction! (I wish I could say that instead of confronting her, I prayed that God would convict her, she confessed, and in response I led her to Christ. But I didn't. I became extremely angry instead.) "How could she do that to me? I trusted her!" I immediately fired her.

I later realized that her addiction to prescription pain-killers began after her shoulder was dislocated from a car accident. The pain-killers allowed her to go back to work shortly after her injury, so she could support herself. Eventually the addiction became more extensive and expensive, and she lost her home as a result.

I thought about the pain she must have suffered. I recalled how she had taken good care of me, despite everything. And I thought about the jewelry she pawned! I couldn't wear those rings anyway, because I can't feel my fingers and the rings fall off. So, I assumed they were still in my jewelry box, safe and sound. Suddenly, I felt compassion for her. I'm not excusing her behavior. What she did was wrong, and she suffered the consequences. She felt very badly about betraying our trust, and later managed to recover and return my wedding ring. Months later, a friend told me that she had recovered from her addiction, was working in the cafeteria of a hospital, had given her life to Christ, and was now attending church. God somehow healed my wounded heart and healed her in the process as well!

We cannot expect to go through life unharmed, but when we forgive, we actually free ourselves from the pain the abuse caused. When others hurt us, we become bitter and angry. Like poison, bitterness enters our bloodstream and slowly consumes our energy, depletes our creativity, and holds us captive. Dwelling on resentments and temptations to revenge can lead to hatred, and eventually affect our whole outlook on life. God wants to set us free from the captivity of bitterness and the darkness of resentment, so we can walk in peace. Forgiveness is the catalyst that frees us from our self-created prisons. We may not be able to forget the memories, but we must not allow the experiences of the past to dominate our future, and control our attitudes and behavior.

The person who caused the past abuse may be a family member, a spouse, or perhaps a deceased parent whom we need to forgive. It was not difficult for me to forgive my caregiver, but some wounds are much older, much deeper and more painful.

I was invited to give my testimony at a Women's Aglow meeting, a women's organization and fellowship group. After I finished my speech, a woman came up to pray for me. Later, I had the privilege of hearing her story.

She was from Rwanda. A Tutsi herself, she had married a Hutu. They were living in America when the 1994 genocide in Rwanda began. She later heard that all her family members, her mother, her father, all her sisters, and brother were, one by one, killed by the members of her husband's tribe! The Rwandan Genocide was the mass killing of close to one million of Rwanda's Tutsis by Hutus tribe in less than 100 days, under the Hutu Power Ideology. It involved neighbors brutally killing neighbors!

The devastation and desperation she must have gone through are beyond my comprehension. Justice against the perpetrators will eventually be served in the highest court of law. In the meantime, how can reconciliation come to a people after such an atrocity? How could they ever live together as neighbors? The most amazing thing is that the country of Rwanda is actively moving towards a genuine process of reconciliation of its people through forgiveness! Many church and governmental programs have been established to facilitate that process.

My friend's wounded heart was not healed until she came to experience the forgiveness and love of God for herself, which in turn allowed her to forgive. In this long and painful process of reconciliation, she has found a new purpose in life. Today, she and her husband both serve as pastors of a Rwandan church, helping others experience reconciliation through forgiveness.

We are in a trying time in this world of chaos. As I am finishing my book, Iran is on the verge of possibly another revolution. I cannot fathom how anyone can cope with the struggles of this life, without the hope that Christ offers. Emotional and spiritual healing is a long process, and we may need the help of a professional. However, knowing that God loves us and has forgiven us, so we can forgive others, is the first step to recovery. There is no healing except in forgiveness.

22

Spiritual Transformation

We are all works in progress

I have vivid memories of being alone one afternoon in the house. It was soon after coming home from the hospital. It was unusual for me to be alone. But that day, no one seemed to be around. I was not comfortable being alone yet; I was afraid of what might go wrong. Cautiously, I wheeled myself into the living room. There was a strange quiet in the air. In my apprehension, I began contemplating on the way things used to be, not so long ago, and a wave of sorrow invaded my soul. Glancing at my hands atrophied from lack of movement, in desperation I cried out loud, "God, look at me, I can't do anything! What can I do now?" It was just a cry of the heart, and I did not expect an answer. Nevertheless, I heard a gentle voice within me saying, "Become like Christ." The answer appalled me more than hearing a voice! In anger I protested, "I'm talking about doing something. What can I do now?" And the voice gently repeated, "Become like Christ."

I had grown accustomed to constantly doing something I perceived to be productive. Yet God seemed to be more interested in me becoming someone, rather than me doing something. To become like Christ! What a daunting task!

Little did I know that conforming to His image was the purpose for our creation. It is an unfinished work throughout our existence on this earth. The Bible calls those who belong to Christ to live by the spirit, and defines the fruit of this spirit as love, joy, peace, patience, kindness, goodness, faithfulness, gentleness, and self-control. But how can our character grow spiritually?

Through this journey of many deep and dark valleys, I have come closer to understanding the role that long suffering has played in my life. Suffering is an inevitable part of life, since we are an imperfect people, living in an imperfect world! Yet suffering is not in vain, otherwise, there would be nothing left but a bitter and terrible experience. Enduring trials is one way we grow spiritually. All of our life experiences will lead us toward this end, but hardship is like an internship in the schooling of life. My husband always says, "You don't learn to ride a bicycle by just reading about it; you must experience it."

When I first became a Christian, I was seeking an experience, a feeling, a sign, a miracle; something to confirm my closeness to God, rather than seeking God Himself. However, God invites us to a relationship with Himself. Christianity at its core is about a "personal relationship with God." In this relationship, when we talk to Him, He listens, and sometimes speaks back; usually in unconventional ways, but we can learn to recognize His ways. It is a relationship that evokes powerful emotions. We can plead, argue, laugh, cry, and even be angry. It is a relationship in which He is no longer a "god" you refer to as "the old man upstairs," but a God who is near, abiding within you, inside your heart.

Through this relationship, a gradual transformation in our soul begins to take place. However, the great lessons in this life are learned during trials, and some lessons are just not learned any other way. We learn to trust God, to see His provision, and to recognize the sufficiency of His sustaining grace. Being physically dependent, I have watched God meet my every need, not necessarily always what I wanted, but always what I needed. Being financially broke after the accident, I have witnessed God's miraculous provision. Step by step, God is teaching me to trust Him, by using different circumstances in my life.

In trials, we also learn about ourselves. Being totally dependent on other people has shown me how selfish, arrogant, demanding, envious, controlling and negative I can be. We must see our wrong attitudes and motives. This is the first and most necessary step to spiritual growth. But the good news is that God wants the abundant love, compassion, generosity, kindness, and goodness in us to be nurtured and revealed. God is more interested in changing us than in just changing our circumstances.

The only thing that is eternal is what we learn here, and the effect it has on our character. We can't take anything else with us. My perspective on life in this world is in actuality preparation for eternal life. I often think, what if a fetus, from its perspective, could wonder about its growing lungs? "What's their purpose, and why do I need them?" Lungs are needed outside the womb for breathing oxygen, but a fetus doesn't understand the purpose of breathing! So it is with some lessons we must learn in this life.

I have my own struggles in certain areas. Sometimes, feeling insecure, I overreact to a particular situation. Or feeling rejected, I confront my resentment and anger. Discouraged, I cry out to God, "Lord, am I even saved? After all that has happened, I'm supposed to be more spiritual, but I'm now worse than before." The reason for this is that I am more aware of my hidden weaknesses. They were always there; I'm just seeing them now! We are all in the process of learning. We are all works in progress.

Yet I have come a long way since those early days of facing paralysis. I remember soon after my accident, riding in my wheelchair in our quiet suburban neighborhood. I would find a secluded area and cry bitterly over what life had chosen to bestow upon me. But now, when I go for a ride in my wheelchair in the neighborhood with Ginger, my sweet toy poodle, I notice every flower, enjoy the warmth of the sun on my face, sense the cool breeze, listen to the chirping of the birds, and I smile and talk to my neighbors. And you know what? Being in a wheelchair doesn't bother me anymore! I can race through a mall and visit all the shops without even getting tired!

I finally understand why the Bible tells us to rejoice in our suffering. During trials, our natural impulse is to become bitter and angry, and to turn away from God. But what we need is a paradigm shift to view trials as the catalysts for change. YES, it is counter-intuitive, but if we view it from a Godly perspective, we can then celebrate our changed character, our awakened heart of compassion, our renewed gentle spirit, and our new freedom. Let's be glad, and shout that we are imperfect humans that God can transform into wonderful, beautiful and extraordinary people. I am grateful, not for the tragedy, but for the resulting insight, character and strength gained from it.

23

Finding Meaning and Purpose

*We are called by God to be a light in the
darkness, and to make this world a little better
for one person at a time.*

"Father, you have given each of us a testimony to your faithfulness, sustaining power, and grace. And it is only with your grace that I can do anything. So I pray that you speak through me to touch the hearts of your people."

This was my prayer, as many people invited me to share my testimony at their churches, women's groups, and various events.

The first time I gave my testimony, I was at the Valley Iranian Church in California. It was the first time after my accident that I traveled by plane. The flight was complicated. They placed me in a regular seat, and my wheelchair was transferred as luggage. Needless to say, my wheelchair was damaged, but I managed. The majority of airlines are now better equipped to cater to someone traveling in a wheelchair. I pray that the day will come when I can fly while sitting in my wheelchair!

As we rode in the taxi cab on the way to the church, Shahriar and my husband began to write lyrics to a beautiful song that we sang in the service at church. When the music faded away, I began speaking. "My story is a story of God's faithfulness," I said, not sure what kind of reaction I would get from people as they heard my testimony about suffering. But I saw tears in the eyes of old men, and hope in the faces of young women. A gentleman approached me afterward, and offered me a large advance to display my paintings for sale in his art gallery!

I was also invited to a community art club to show my art, and to teach those with physical limitations to paint. Painting is very therapeutic in helping people use their creativity and in expressing themselves. People often tell me about their despair, and then they tell me that I give them hope! I can't think of a better way to use my talent and energy than to help inspire those in my circle of influence.

Viktor Frankl, a psychiatrist and a Holocaust survivor, indicated in his book, *Man's Search for Meaning*, that we can choose to cope with suffering, find meaning in it, and move forward with renewed purpose. Living with paralysis for years, I have come to realize that when we find a purpose for our suffering, it suddenly becomes tolerable. Finding a greater cause, something more important than ourselves, will give our lives a new meaning. Many people have helped me in tangible ways when I was most vulnerable; and now, I want to help others in their time of greatest need. This desire to help others is not from obligation or duty, but rather from love and commitment. But there is much work to be done, and few workers. Lord, please send the workers. There's a lot of work to be done!

One night we were invited to a friend's house for dinner. Another couple was also invited. They were in their late sixties. They seemed active, wealthy and well traveled. I sensed a little discomfort on their part, and I assumed it was due to my paralysis. After dinner we sat by the fireplace, and conversations became more personal. They told me that they had parented two daughters. One was killed in an automobile accident, and the other one died from ALS a few years ago, leaving their two grandsons to be raised by their son-in-law. Now, this couple's only grandsons were suffering from ALS, and soon had to face a life of being in a wheelchair!

ALS, often referred to as "Lou Gehrig's Disease," is a progressive neuro-degenerative disease that affects nerve cells in the brain and the spinal cord. Normally, motor neurons signal from the brain to the spinal cord and from the spinal cord to the muscles throughout the body. ALS causes the progressive degeneration of those motor neurons, which slowly and inevitably leads to complete paralysis and death.

And I thought their discomfort had something to do with me personally! (Another example of dysfunctional thoughts; we tend to think others are behaving negatively because of us when in fact it has nothing to do with us personally.) My wheelchair was just a reminder of the future their grandsons were facing. They were only 20 and 23 years old. My heart went out to them. How could I help? Could I talk to them and give them some kind of hope? Could I form a group to help them make the necessary changes to their house? I wanted to cry out, "How can I help?" There is much work to be done, but few workers. Lord, please send the workers. There's a lot of work to be done!

A friend called me the other day. I hadn't spoken to her for some time. I asked how she was doing. In a fatigued voice, she said that she was alone and depressed. She had recently been diagnosed with rheumatoid arthritis, and was now going through chemotherapy to reduce the debilitating symptoms. She said that some days, she couldn't even get out of bed to fix herself a meal. She is only in her thirties!

There is no known cure for rheumatoid arthritis. It is an auto-immune disease that causes chronic inflammation of the joints where the body's tissues are mistakenly attacked by its own immune system. It is an extremely painful disease, which can lead to joint destruction and deformity.

She had no children; her husband was out of town looking for a job, and all her relatives lived in Iran. My heart went out to her. I wanted to cry out, "How can I help?" I listened to her, encouraged her, prayed with her and gave her hope, but there is much work to be done, and only a few workers. Lord, please send the workers. There's a lot of work to be done!

We are called by God to be a light in the darkness, and to make this world a little better for one person at a time. If we could just help the people around us, and not be so concerned with the size or the scope of our service, we can make a difference in our world. We cannot feel totally fulfilled without serving others. I am most unhappy when I am consumed with only myself and my desires. When I am self-centered and prideful, I feel the heaviness of shackles holding me in bondage. I lose my freedom—freedom to love, to share, and to laugh. But I am also keenly aware that I can only relate to others' pains to the extent that I have experienced it myself.

My suffering was not in vain after all! I have changed from a totally self-absorbed person to a person more concerned with others; from being insensitive towards others' needs, to being more aware of others' shattered dreams. A new sense of purpose and a new life has emerged that has proven to be more meaningful than the world I left behind. I now have a group of friends whom I can call whenever a need to help others arises. In the same way that I received tangible help in times of my greatest need, together we have helped many in times of their greatest need.

As you have heard, God uses our miseries by turning them into ministries! Although each life is different, each of us has been given a divine purpose to fulfill in this life. God will inspire you to do His will for His purposes. He will give you the desires of your heart. God will help you to discover your gifts and talents, and put you in touch with just the right people to make it all happen. As a piece of the puzzle, we must find our position in the final picture, in which the strands are woven together in such a way as to form a beautiful tapestry.

This powerful prayer of Saint Francis gives us a beautiful example of how God inspires us to do His will.

Prayer of Saint Francis of Assisi

Lord, make me an instrument of your peace.
Where there is hatred, let me sow love;
where there is injury, pardon;
where there is doubt, faith;
where there is despair, hope;
where there is darkness, light;
and where there is sadness, joy.
O Divine Master, grant that I may not so much seek
to be consoled as to console;
to be understood as to understand;
to be loved as to love.
For it is in giving that we receive;
it is in pardoning that we are pardoned;
and it is in dying that we are born to eternal life.

Amen

24

Real Freedom

"You will know the truth,
and the truth will set you free."

John 8:32

Jesus promises a certain kind of freedom. *"You will know the truth, and the truth will set you free."* John 8:32.

> He promises to free us from our guilt and shame, by His forgiveness.
> He frees us from our worries, with His promise of a peace that surpasses all human understanding.
> He frees us from our fears, by His assurance of everlasting life.

This freedom offers a state of tranquility in the middle of our difficult circumstances. It is not the absence of problems, but the ability to cope with a peace of mind, believing that all things work together for good for those who love God and are called according to His plan. We don't know how "all things work for good", but I know that in my case, I had to look at things from a Godly perspective. And only then was I able to see the "good," and began to see the miracles around me.

This freedom gives us the ability to make good choices. When tragedy strikes in the middle of the night, and our world suddenly turns upside down, we face choices. Of course, we will confront disappointment, anger, or depression, but we must not let it consume us. We must make a conscious decision to let go, and to instead choose love, peace, forgiveness, and trust. Every day, I am faced with these difficult decisions to choose what the Word of God calls death or life,

> bitterness or forgiveness,
> anger or acceptance,
> self-pity or forgetting the past.

And with each good choice I make, the closer I am to becoming more loving, joyful, and free. And on those mornings when I don't want to face my day, I take my husband's advice! I begin by meditating on the fact that I am beloved by God. I rejoice in this day, because it is the only one I can do anything about. And I remind myself that I have everything I need to be happy this day, by meditating on the positive aspects of my life.

We go through life not knowing the future, but if we trust God and know that He can change a meaningless life into something beautiful, we experience peace, despite our circumstances. This is the perspective I try to have when I face yet another hurdle. My hope in writing this book is that you may find this freedom and peace, despite your circumstances. I don't pretend to know all the answers, but one thing I am certain of; our suffering has a higher purpose and meaning, because God wants to give us something much more valuable than what we have lost.

We are in a spiritual battle. The Bible calls it a warfare between the flesh and the spirit. It requires alertness, perseverance and commitment. The road is long, but the view from the mountain-top is breathtaking.

I see a magnificently strong stallion in his shiny coat, with shackles around his ankles, holding him captive in a dark dungeon. Fleeing to freedom, he breaks the iron chains of the shackles, and runs through the deep and dark forest: trotting between trees, dodging the thick tree branches, never looking back! Aware of the predators in his surroundings, with agility and alertness, he leaps over bushes and hurdles, until he reaches a wide-open terrain. The remnants of the heavy shackles cutting into his ankles have weighed him down. Even so, he continues to run at greater speed until the shackles are loosened, and one by one they break off and fall as he finally reaches the mountain-top overlooking the horizon. He comes to a halt, with steam blowing from his nostrils, he gazes at the majestic horizon at a distance. The sun is rising. Free at last! Free at last!

25

Healing

Inner joy is in our hearts, and it is a state of mind.

I recall the days in the hospital, waking up in the morning and seeing Bill sitting in a chair across from my bed. Bill Cleaton was his name. In his seventies, he was one of the founders and the oldest member of our church. Bill had a wonderful singing voice. He would sing to me in the hospital, read to me, and attempt to answer the profound questions with which I struggled. I have yet to meet a more faithful servant of God.

On one afternoon in early spring, I remember being in the "garden" at the hospital. The day was bright with blue sky. The hospital volunteers had brought puppies to the garden for the patients to play with. One volunteer placed a fluffy, furry, adorable puppy on my lap. I couldn't feel the puppy's weight, or its warmth against my body. It was a sad realization! In a complete paralysis, there is no feeling below the point of injury.

Bill had joined me in the garden that day. It was a serene place for conversing. I asked him about his thoughts on miraculous healing. I had heard of many Christians being miraculously healed by God; I didn't know what to think about that now. His reply was that God still heals miraculously, but it is no longer His usual method.

It wasn't quite the answer I wanted to hear at the time. I longed to be healed miraculously, to be as I was before. After all, God is able to heal! The doctors can tell you how many healings they have witnessed that can only be explained by a miracle! Somehow, I felt I should be treated special by God. Somehow, I felt different from others who were facing similar misfortunes. I deserved a different destiny than the carpenter lying in the hospital room next door, who became paralyzed as a result of falling off his ladder. I deserved a different destiny from the paralyzed teenager lying in the other room, who had been driving while intoxicated. Somehow, I felt I deserved a special place in the universe, and a different destiny.

Fueled by well-meaning Christians, miraculous healing had become an obsession with me. I was extremely vulnerable at that time, and was willing to hang on to any sign that might provide some hope for my healing. For a long time, I was reluctant to part with my old clothes because secretly, I believed that one day I would be able to wear all those tight suits and high heel shoes again.

But I have come to accept that even without my physical healing, I can be whole, complete and happy. I realize that a lot has been taken away from me; many of the senses that used to bring me pleasure and joy. However, I have gained much more in return; a joy and a peace that does not come from things, places, or even people, but only from God. This joy can never be taken away from me.

I recently watched a documentary about blind children attending schools for the blind. One child's comment was, "I am blind, but my heart is not blind. The seeing people's hearts are blind. I am happy!" He had found a source of inner joy. He had discovered that although he is not able to see with his eyes, he could behold with his heart. In the same way, although I may never walk on this earth, perhaps I could learn to fly, because inner joy is in our hearts, and it is a state of mind. That's real healing.

There is also another aspect to my contentment with my circumstances. All physical healing is temporary on this earth, because death is quietly lurking in the shadows. I'm no longer afraid of death, because I know where I'm going . . . but in the words of Woody Allen, "I just don't wanna' be there when it happens!"

My focus is no longer just on me being physically healed, because I believe one day my healed spirit will have a heavenly body that will not be subjected to disease and decay. Our beliefs have a profound impact on how we respond to the things that happen to us, and my hope is no longer just about what happens in this world.

It has taken me a long time to understand what Bill was trying to tell me, on that sunny afternoon in the hospital. I am not physically healed, but through my faith in Christ and the wisdom of many writers whose teachings helped to heal my thoughts and emotions, I have come to accept, adapt and find new meaning in life.

Bill touched the lives of many by his love, compassion, and faith. Bill passed away in 2011, but in our hearts, he will always remain.

26

The Reason for My Hope

My best years are not behind me,
but they are yet to come!

As a child, I remember looking through a kaleidoscope for the first time, seeing the array of colorful patterns created by the light reflected on the beads, pebbles, and bits of glass on a circle of mirrors. I was in awe and wonder, thinking this must be what heaven is like—light, colors, beauty, and serenity.

I still think about heaven, dreaming of traveling over still waters to a distant land. All my cares and anxieties slip away as I arrive at a place of complete peace, pure love, total security, and unspeakable joy. A place where the flowers are always in bloom, rivers are flowing with crystal clear waters, and the air is soft and cool. A place of no impurity and no decay, where gardens of herbs, vegetables, and fruits of all kinds are tended not by the sweat-of the-brow, but by the energy and wisdom of God. A place where work and play are not separated; and children are laughing and playing in a community of people in complete serenity, with pure hearts filled with love for one another. There is no need for the sun, because the light of God illuminates this place. We will be permanently living in the joy of the presence of God.

There will be no more tears, sorrow, wars, pain or death. I want you to join me there, so that together we can dance to the heavenly songs of the angels.

I have a real hope that my journey in this life is leading me to my eternal destiny. In fact, our journey to heaven begins the moment we give our hearts to Jesus. It begins with the restoration of our spirit, our soul, our body and ultimately our world. It is not the name "Christian" that saves us, but the Spirit of Christ within us. I believe that heaven is more than just a place; it is a particular state of mind. It is a mind that has been set free.

Carrying the songs of heaven in my heart has allowed me to focus on my purpose, rather than on what life has withheld from me. And during the storms of life, I am assured that all things are leading me to the right destination.

At the time he wrote *Still Me,* Christopher Reeve, truly my hero, indicated that he believed his best years were behind him. But I have a different view. My best years are not behind me, but they are yet to come! My hope extends beyond my worldly existence. Heaven is my home and my destiny. It is not free. By dying on the cross, Christ paid a high price for my freedom, a very high price indeed.

Change in life is inevitable. Jesus said that in this world we will have troubles. But all of this just makes us realize how much we need God, and awakens us to desire Him above all, because He is the unchanging source of hope. God will empower us to go through the storms of life. In the meantime, our capacity to love will increase through these experiences. God wants us to learn to love, before He takes us to a place where the law of the land is love. And in this world, we are being prepared for this everlasting life, as the love and compassion of Christ cleanses our hearts.

To live the life that Jesus teaches, we need the empowerment from His Spirit. The longer I live as a Christian, the more I realize how easily I can revert to my old ways of thinking, and my old nature. Every day, I need the power of His Spirit within me, to live the life that Jesus taught. In the same way, you can be empowered. God has given us free will, and He will not violate that. He has chosen us, but are we willing to choose Him? If you seek Him, you will find Him. He is the answer to your life-long questions.

I found this note in my journal from years ago. I don't know who wrote it, but it is rephrased from Isaiah 61:1.

> *"His hand reaches into the depths of the earth; He can reach also to you. He hasn't come to condemn the world, but to save the world. He hasn't come to accuse the imprisoned, but to set the captives free."*

He wants to set you free!

Epilogue

I look back in wonder, grateful for what God has done for me! With His grace and special ways He has revealed His love to me, and with the support of others, I have overcome many obstacles. God continues to do miracles in my life through the people I meet. What happened to me not only changed me, but also changed the world around me.

Today is December 26th. On this Christmas morning I called all the members of my family to wish them a Merry Christmas. I called my sister, Simin whom I haven't seen for many years. She lives in Los Angeles. Our paths drifted apart but not our hearts, I have prayed for her for many years. She was ecstatic to hear from me! Through the weeping and sobbing, I learned that she had been receiving text messages from a friend, Bible Scriptures that pertained to difficult circumstances she had been experiencing in her life. She knew the messages were the voice of God calling her, and I was reminded of a promise made to me, long ago. *"Man ghom e to ra nejat khaham dad." (I will save your people).* I will wait for that day!

Iran is a country in crisis. Iranians facing shattered dreams are open to the hope that only Jesus offers. My prayer is that every Iranian would one day have the freedom to worship Jesus Christ as their Savior.

This is the painting I did of the image I saw in the hospital.
God was whispering, *"I am here, I am with you, I am carrying you."*

Painting with my hand brace

Nasrin in her studio

Want to Learn more about Christian Faith?

Recommended Books

Mere Christianity, by C. S. Lewis

C. S. Lewis, a distinguished professor of literature at Oxford and Cambridge Universities who grew up as an atheist, later converts to Christianity. Author of numerous books, Mere Christianity is perhaps the most influential Christian book of the twentieth century. The book begins by presenting what has often been called the moral argument for the existence of God. In order to understand Christianity, one must understand the moral law, which is the underlying structure of the universe. Unless one grasps the dismay which comes from humanity's failure to keep the moral law, one cannot understand the coming of Christ and his work.

Letters from a Skeptic: A Son Wrestles with his Father's Questions about Christianity, by Gregory A. Boyd, Edward Boyd

When Greg Boyd became a Christian, his agnostic father thought he had joined a cult. This book is a collection of letters from Greg to his father, Ed, to attempt to answer his doubts and questions about the validity of the Christian views. This best-selling book is honest, thought-stimulating and intelligent. It has become a classic. Dr. Boyd has M.Div from Yale Divinity School and a PhD from Princeton Theological Seminary. Dr. Greg has also published numerous books and is a speaker on the international scene.

The Case for Christ: A Journalist's Personal Investigation of the Evidence for Jesus, by Lee Strobel

Lee Strobel, an attorney, former legal editor of The Chicago Tribune and an award-winning journalist—began his two-year search for evidence regarding the credibility of Christianity after his wife's sudden conversion. An atheist, he became genuinely curious about her faith because he had seen positive changes in his wife during the months following her conversion (which she attributed to God). Exhaustively studying the historical data surrounding Christ's death and resurrection for nearly two years, Strobel found evidence after evidence, which supported not only Jesus' life but his actual resurrection as well.